WILD PORTRAITS

WILD PORTRAITS

The Wildlife Art of
Raymond Harris-Ching

Text by Peter Hansard

Foreword by the Hon. A. D. Tryon

Airlife
England

Other books from Raymond Harris-Ching

Book of British Birds
The Bird Paintings
Studies and Sketches of a Bird Painter
The Art of Raymond Ching
New Zealand Birds, An Artist's Field Studies

Copyright © Raymond Harris-Ching 1988

First published in Great Britain in 1988
by Airlife Publishing Ltd

ISBN 1 85310 041 2

All rights reserved. No part of this publication may be reproduced, stored or introduced into a retrieval system, or transmitted in any form or by any means (electronic, mechanical, photocopying, recording or otherwise), without the prior written permission of the copyright owners, except for brief passages quoted by a reviewer in a newspaper or magazine.

Typeset by Jacobsons, Auckland
Book production by Phillip Ridge/Bookmakers, Auckland
Printed by Everbest Printing Co. Ltd, Hong Kong

This book may not be reproduced in any manner or the pages or artwork applied to any materials listed but not limited to the following:
Cut, trimmed or sized to alter the existing trim size of the pages.
Laminated, transferred or applied to any substance, form or surface.
Carved, moulded or formed in any manner in any material.
Lifted or removed chemically or by any other means, or transferred to produce slides or transparencies.
Used as promotional aids, premiums, or advertising or for non-profit or educational purposes.
Engraved, embossed, etched or copied by any means onto any surface whether metallic, foil, transparent or translucent.
Matted or framed with the intent to create other products for sale or re-sale or profit in any manner whatsoever, without express written consent from Raymond Harris-Ching, c/o SéTo Publishing, PO Box 4028, Auckland, New Zealand.

Airlife Publishing Ltd.
7 St John's Hill, Shrewsbury SY1 1JE

'I have no idea whether or not my vision of the natural world might coincide with anybody else's view of things, but I've been drawing, more or less obsessively, for thirty years to try to show what I've made of it.'

RAYMOND HARRIS-CHING, 1987

The Publisher would like to thank the following people for their support and interest in this book: Carol Sinclair-Smith, Tanya Lock, The Hon. D. E. H. Bigham and the staff of The Tryon Gallery, Colette Harris-Ching, Jaan Voot, Bill Double, Jay Whitcombe, Warwick Woodward and the many collectors and galleries who made original artworks in their possession available for reproduction.

FRONTISPIECE:
Camel study   oil   29.2 x 31.8 cm   (11½ x 12½")   1984

PAGE 5:
Rufous night heron   *Nycticorax caledonicus*   oil   38.1 x 48.3 cm   (15 x 19")   1985

PAGE 7:
Pacific gull   *Larus pacificus*   (detail) oil   48.3 x 35.6 cm   (19 x 14")   1981

PAGE 9:
Barn owl   *Tyto alba*   watercolour and gouache   71.8 x 53.3 cm   (28¼ x 21")   1975

RIGHT:
Platypus   *Ornithorhynchus anatinus*   oil   55.9 x 66 cm   (22 x 26")   1987

PAGE 12:
Diana monkey   *Cercopithecus diana*   oil   36.8 x 30.5 cm   (14½ x 12")   1980

PAGE 14:
White-cheeked honeyeaters 'on wattle'   *Phylidonyris nigra*   oil   35.6 x 48.3 cm   (14 x 19")   1987

PAGE 30:
The triptych   oil on panels   111.8 x 215.4 cm   (44 x 84")   1984

PAGE 48:
Red-crowned parakeet chicks   *Cyanoramphus novaezelandiae*   oil   29.2 x 14 cm   (11½ x 5½")   1985

Contents

Foreword	15
Introduction	17
The Gilded Triptych	31
The Plates	49
Exhibitions	213
Bibliography	214
Index	215

Foreword

In 1977 Raymond Harris-Ching asked me to write the foreword to his book *The Bird Paintings*. Since then further books featuring other aspects of his work have been published, including *Studies and Sketches of a Bird Painter, The Art of Raymond Ching,* and recently *New Zealand Birds,* which includes some birds so rare that many of the sketches from life were the first of their kind to appear. He is presently working on a monograph of the kiwi, the plates for which have already caused much excitement in anticipation of their completion.

Now I have been asked to write a foreword to this fine volume, *Wild Portraits,* which I am particularly pleased to do since it includes a wealth of the artist's studies from his native New Zealand, Australia, America, Africa, England and many other parts of the world. The subjects vary from lions to wrens!

Since 1977 Ray's work has become increasingly known, collected and admired by a worldwide public and I feel justified to repeat that he has indeed 'brought a new dimension to bird portraiture'; I would also add that his sensitive and delicate portrayal of birds and mammals such as the monkeys has seldom been surpassed.

We are fortunate that such a fine artist should choose to record the extraordinarily diverse animal life of our world and allow us, in these painted studies, the pleasure of his exquisite draughtsmanship.

Aylmer Tryon
London, 1987

ABOVE: Harris-Ching in the studio

Introduction

Imagine a painter's studio. The painter sits at his easel and draws or paints a dead bird lying on his table. The bird is only recently dead, its feathers glowing in a shaft of filtered light from the window. The dark, half-closed eye still shows a bright pin-point of luminescence, the ceres are still full with the colours of life. The painter works quickly. As with any 'life' study, he knows his subject is of a transient nature because all too soon the processes of decay will change what he sees, just as he knows a human model cannot hold a pose indefinitely and that once lost, it is never again quite the same.

This knowledge adds tension, challenge, uncertainty, pressure and a vital edge to his painting. Passion, to a greater or lesser extent, and depending upon the painter, enters the picture.

Of course, the painter knows his subject. But this bird, on this table, on this day, is unique. It's something he has never seen before because it's a combination of textures, form and colours, bathed in a quality of light existing only for that day, that particular afternoon, say, and maybe for just half an hour before the sun goes down and the whole appearance of his subject is markedly altered. Not only that, certain tricks of the light soon become evident. Black feathers catching the sun's rays at an oblique angle appear almost silver or pearly grey. Some of the deep shadows are not black at all but a peculiar bluish-brown. And what colour, really, are the long thin distorted shadows cast upon the tabletop by outflung primaries in the wing?

No wonder the painter wants to concentrate. No wonder he wants privacy. No wonder his dead bird is all that matters.

And our painter could be anyone who has ever undertaken to make such a picture during the last 500 years.

But wait a moment. Not *anyone* surely? The contemporary painter can take a photograph to use as reference, can't he? The point of photography, the very reason it's been of such interest to painters since its invention, is that it 'captures' such a scene and in so doing (given correct exposure and pin-sharp focus), freezes the subject, exactly the way it is at that moment, for all time.

Suppose then, our modern painter doesn't bother with the dead bird as an immediate subject for his painting, but instead spends twenty minutes or so arranging it nicely by the window, photographs it and then buries it in the backyard. He still faces the same problems with his painting, he still has to work it all out, but one vital change takes place in his attitude to the painting. He will still want to get on with it and he'll look forward to getting his photographs back from the processors with much eagerness. But now he has *time*. Time to face up to the challenge. Time to analyse the image at leisure, to have a cup of coffee or light a cigarette, to drop the car off at the garage. Time to work things out. A kind of detached rationality replaces some of the nervous pressure (and therefore some of the passion), previously such an integral part of the process when working from the real thing.

One wonders, however, whether this photographic liberation, though tempting, is in the best interests of the animal painter. Perhaps not. Certainly, it is pleasing to note Ray Harris-Ching's greater emphasis on bird and mammal studies directly painted and in the form of 'portraits'.

The reproductions in this book cover a range of wild creatures from many parts of the world. Although the plates follow more or less a geographical sequence, any rigid taxonomic or other speciological format has been avoided. This has been done because Ray Harris-Ching is most usually concerned with the *individual* qualities of any given animal and, as far as the paintings chosen for this book are concerned, habitat or larger environmental considerations are not the major issue. As well, many of the works reproduced here are study sketches; they often represent the very best of his paintings, and in the normal course of events many would otherwise remain unpublished.

In other words, this book is primarily about Ray's paintings and only incidentally about the wildlife he has painted.

ABOVE:
Charley Barley   watercolour
67 x 55 cm   (26½ x 21½")   1975

RIGHT:
Botany Bay
gouache   66 x 53 cm   (26 x 21")   1976

ABOVE: Vanessa   watercolour   66 x 53 cm   (26 x 21")   1978

For that reason, the notes on the various species portrayed have been confined to the text accompanying each plate. Here, then, in these introductory pages, let us concern ourselves only with a look at that peculiar universe in which Ray has lived all of his adult life — a compulsive and often obsessive world revolving around the constant pursuit of paintings.

If environmental considerations do not play a great part in these paintings, then it's interesting that they should occupy such an important role in Ray's own everyday life. One of the reasons he spends so much time travelling, and why he likes to work alternately from studios on opposite sides of the world, has been his incessant need for change, for the stimulation and experience of contrasting landscapes.

It is appropriate, therefore, to begin with Australia — not necessarily because Ray lives there from time to time — but more because it's a uniquely neutral ground, neither the New Zealand of his birth nor the Britain in which he normally resides, but a completely separate country which has fascinated him for many years.

One of the great perplexities of wildlife painting is that although Australia offers naturalists and painters some of the most interesting and remarkable species seen anywhere, this wonderfully varied wealth of natural subjects seems largely ignored by most eminent wildlife artists living outside that country.

It's quite common for internationally known painters of this genre to travel extensively, from Amazonian jungles to Antarctica, but for some reason the huge variety of endemic Australian fauna (unlike that of Africa for instance) fails to attract their interest.

Of course, Australian animals are not normally regarded as 'game' species and even today, following nineteenth-century tradition, much wildlife art has grown out of, and remains loosely associated with, hunting interests. Such interests are now, by the way, instigating many of the most successful conservation programmes of recent years.

If these Australian species, particularly the mammals, are not generally perceived as especially important to the international painter, then it follows that Australian wildlife painting doesn't

receive wide acclaim. I don't necessarily wish to involve myself in the ins and outs of any such argument here — all I do know is that it's entirely typical of Ray that wallabies and wombats should have proven to be an integral part of his obsessive interest in Australian fauna and that such species, no matter what anyone else may have to say about them, significantly occupy his attention and now form the greater part of his output.

For whatever reasons, Ray is increasingly preoccupied with thoughts of that continent, and there is no doubt it's the kind of place that seems to come up with the goods as far as he is concerned. By driving virtually in any direction for just a few days, he can easily find enough material to fill his sketchbook or a couple of rolls of film, and thereby provide himself with the raw subject-matter for months of work. On more extended field trips, with the practical help of naturalist friends, he has found it possible to assemble an enormous collection of drawings and oil sketches, to be shipped back to the studio for development later into completed works. Ray survives these brief but potentially dangerous forays into the fringes of the outback by closely following advice on survival from anyone who will give it or, best of all, by accompanying a natural history museum collecting expedition.

I have always been struck by one instance, occasioned by a visit Ray made to the art writer and scientist, Allan McEvey, Emeritus Curator of Birds, National Museum of Victoria. While examining the museum's splendid nineteenth-century display housing a comprehensive collection of Australian bird eggs, McEvey happened to remark that the eggs, nestling in cottonwool in their trays, were subject to constant, if minor, vibrations from passing pedestrian and motor traffic, and that it was his observation that these barely measurable tremors resulted in the eggs turning completely upon their axis, once every twenty-three years!

This is the kind of comment which Ray finds simply staggering, mainly because it pre-supposes that the observer, quite naturally and in the normal course of events, will expect to be on the spot for that period of time, in order to be able to make such a marvellously unhurried and accurate day-to-day observation in the first place.

Ray envies this kind of ordered routine, so essential to academic and scientific method, but it could not contrast more sharply with his nature. It points to a real dilemma in his life: that although his impulse is just to get on with making paintings, the absolute requirement of wildlife art, with its demands of accuracy and insistence upon precise order, has required him to adopt many of the scientist's disciplines.

The study sketch is his *metier*. Study sketches are all about drawing, about getting it down right, about seeing it as light and shade in paint, working it out in an immediate, unplanned way. This seems to be the life blood of Ray's painting and demonstrates his true skills as a draughtsman in paint.

Moreover, such carefully observed sketches suit Ray's method of working. With either watercolours or very thin oils and a drying agent, he is still able by means of the study sketch to compile a collection of work while travelling. Developing more detailed and finished compositions (and waiting about for the various layers of paint to dry) is more obviously better left to those few months of the year when he is at home and working on studio paintings.

'Home' usually means either England or New Zealand. Like Australia, the land of his birth exerts a strong emotional pull on Ray although such unaccountable tugs of homesickness, or whatever else they might be, are at their strongest when furtherest away from the place! If domiciled in New Zealand or Australia, Ray's thoughts will sooner or later (usually sooner) return to life and work in Europe — and so the cycle goes.

One of the side effects of this constant upheaval is the rather incomplete and primitive studio set-ups in which Ray seems content to paint. For an artist of his calibre and reputation, his working conditions seem by any standards, limited and chaotic. After a while, one realises that most of the difficulties Ray experiences in the studio (as in life), are entirely of his own making, or at least tend to come about as a result of his surprisingly unanalytical mind — unanalytical that is, so far as anything to do with the technical side of painting goes, or, indeed, as far as technology in a much wider sense, is concerned.

ABOVE:
In the Grampian Mountains of Victoria, an echidna burrows away to hide under leaves and frustrate any serious attempt at sketching. The spirit of the area will be remembered by the artist and the site of the little animal's 'nest' carefully measured and drawn for a painting to be developed at a later date.

LEFT:
The artist searching out koalas in the You-Yangs. Just days after this sketching trip, 120°F temperatures and hot winds from the interior set this area alight and reduced the flora and fauna portrayed in the drawings to ashes.

LEFT:
Red wattlebird   *Anthochaera carunculata*
pencil   50.8 x 35.6 cm   (20 x 14")   1984

ABOVE:
Brush-turkey   *Alectura lathami*
pencil   50.8 x 36.8 cm   (20 x 14½")   1984

This stubborn or in-built unwillingness even to consider such matters probably inconveniences no one so much as Ray himself.

I remember his concern many years ago at the amount of dust persistently adhering to the wet surface of his paintings. Ray would haunt the great national collections in London, puzzled at finding no such problem in evidence on paintings by the likes of Van Eyck or Holbein. Then, at home in his Blackheath studio (where no cleaner was allowed entry) he'd pace up and down in the very heights of nervous frustration, filling the air with great clouds of dust and ash as he walked through huge piles of old cigarette ends! In those days (at least twenty years ago), Ray smoked so heavily that he actually managed to create mounds of cigarette butts some two feet high in rows against the studio walls.

It was his — quite unique — observation that such awful heaps of butts could only reach this height and no higher before slipping, sliding or spilling outwards across the floor towards his easel. Admittedly, he smoked only a quarter of any cigarette before dunking it in his water-jar, so they were rather long butts. Sadly, however, this is not the kind of observation to rock the scientific world, nor is it such a pleasant diversion as Allan McEvey's eggs!

Nevertheless, it is absolutely true to say that Ray unaccountably failed for some time to consider seriously the connection between impatiently discarded cigarettes and the dust on his paintings. Later, after reading of such painters as Lawrence Alma-Tadema or Sir Gerald Kelly, who wore long dust coats and had their studios swept and watered every day before commencing work, Ray began a huge spring-clean.

But clutter remains and the conglomeration of fascinating but unrelated articles crammed into any available shelf, the spread of page-designs and pencil drawings strewn over the floor, the huge adjoining library of thousands of volumes all specifically relating to birds, help add to an almost overwhelming aura of feverish work in progress. Ray is a compulsive worker, and deprived of work opportunities he often appears frustrated beyond measure.

This is all the more reason why Ray should think seriously about getting his studio properly set up. After twenty years of half-hearted attempts, he admits that it is unlikely he ever will. Where other painters make use of an amazing selection of modern equipment — hydraulically controlled drawing boards that shift position at the touch of a finger, daylight balanced lighting, perfect lumbar-support chairs — Ray hammers a couple of nails into his easel to support whichever painting he's working on and then pulls them out to reposition them for the next picture. He works under the 75 watt bulb of an ordinary desk lamp, all the while perched on an uncomfortable but beautiful eighteenth-century chair.

From time to time he concedes that life would be better if he did adopt a more practical approach. At least two leading wildlife painters have lent their weight to this suggestion. Robert Bateman, while on a visit, expressed amazement at the difficulties Ray ignores, and offered advice by explaining his own layout and, moreover, offered detailed and comprehensive sketches to show Ray how he too might achieve a similar lighting configuration.

George McLean, staying over at the studio one Christmas, was equally astonished at Ray's working conditions. Shrewdly realising what he was up against, McLean, not a man to mess about, persuaded his wife Helen to include an actual lighting set-up (daylight balanced and all that sort of thing) in her luggage when she next visited Britain. Today, the self-same lamp still sits in its box, in unused pristine condition.

Why hasn't he wired it up then? 'Because,' Ray explains, 'if I get the plugs wrong, as I probably would, I'd only succeed in blowing up George's beautiful lamp — and I couldn't bear having to tell him that.'

Obviously, both Bateman and McLean have failed to comprehend fully that the 'techno-naive' is not yet an entirely extinct species and that in Ray Harris-Ching, they have very probably come up against the archetype.

Meanwhile, Ray steadfastly refuses to spend any time whatsoever on solving the lighting problem, and despite recurrent eye troubles, which limit his sessions at the drawing board, he has yet to organise the local electrician to put the 'McLean lamp' into service.

ABOVE:
Tawny frogmouths *Podargus strigoides*
pencil   53 x 36 cm   (21 x 14")   1984

LEFT:
European blackbird   *Turdus merula*
watercolour   68.6 x 50.8 cm (27 x 20")
1974

RIGHT:
Grey partridges   *Perdix perdix*
watercolour   66.7 x 47 cm (26¼ x 18½")
1972

But what of the actual process of painting — Ray's techniques and his methods? Well, they are simple and direct. In the first place, Ray has always been a superb draughtsman and his paintings rely on this factor, more or less, for much of their impact. Ray's painting technique is very much confined to the task of 'drawing' the paint on, so that, for example, bold washes of colour are almost never used.

The form, texture and 'light' are 'drawn' with the brush in rapid strokes very much like those that might be made with a pencil. Normally, Ray begins with what seems a remarkably detailed and complete drawing carried out on a finely sanded and smoothly gessoed panel. The whole surface is then thinly keyed with an overall, very pale tone, sometimes distressed slightly to give the illusion of texture although always remaining a smooth, transparent coating. From time to time he may put aside the panels in favour of canvas, but for small paintings at any rate, the solidity of a masonite panel probably offers the preferred surface.

ABOVE: 'The Armoury' library

ABOVE LEFT:
'The Armoury'

ABOVE:
The studio's charming stone oriel window, much prized in a medieval house, was set centuries ago with stained glass panes depicting birds — now strangely significant for a painter whose life and work has been so connected with the same subject.

Pigment is applied sparingly, always well thinned so that the actual stroke of paint goes on as a more or less transparent mark. The painting is gradually built up in this way, often with pencil lines and underlying coats of gesso still visible even in finished areas. To Ray, this 'thinness' is of great importance, it's what he strives for most, because for him, it suggests restraint, control, and that just maybe, the paint 'went on right'. He's inclined, therefore, to see any 'overworked' areas as evidence of total failure on his part.

It's all a question of taste, of course, and Ray holds no personal views on the liberal application of impasto used by other painters. But where his own work is concerned, that kind of paint surface just doesn't equate with his own instinctive way of doing things and is not, he knows, even worth his consideration. The thinner, the better.

Through the 1970s, Harris-Ching's paintings were, almost without exception, watercolours. From this decade came many fine portraits, including 'Vanessa' (page 18) and Doug Childs in 'Botany Bay' (page 19). These, along with a small number of highly personal works — 'Charley Barley' (page 18) is one of them — are all dry-brush watercolours. A quick glance will immediately make clear that their creator is in full technical control over their construction. More recently, it has been his contact with works of the nineteenth-century Pre-Raphaelite Brotherhood that has prompted some re-direction, especially, perhaps, in his change to oils as the dominant medium.

Ray acknowledges that his starting point for the corpus of animal paintings and drawings he has so far produced lies firmly within the conventions of 'Wildlife Art', but increasingly the spirit of his work is moving towards the seventeenth-century canvasses of Melchior d' Hondecoeter, and away from the influences of the two great twentieth-century animal painters, Bruno Liljefors and Wilhelm Kuhnert. To separate easily the

ABOVE:
Study-skins and skeletons in the studio.

LEFT:
Studies of razorbill and guillemot
pencil   50.8 x 35.6 cm   (20 x 14")   1986

naturalist from the artist in the work of these latter painters cannot be done — the animal art of Liljefors and Kuhnert could not have been made were they not also fine naturalists. However, in the works of d'Hondecoeter this is not necessarily so, and in fact quite the opposite may hold true. It is here that the seeds for the body of Ray's present output lie. 'In a painting,' he says, 'I have no wish to tell you about the bird's lifestyle . . . I just want to say something of my confrontation with it and what I finally made of it.'

Ray Harris-Ching's painting is becoming increasingly defined; variation of plumage colour and patterns, depth and softness of feathering are, since the late 1970s, at the centre of his work. Hardly anywhere is comment made on a creature's habits, feeding requirements or nesting cycle; seldom now does he attempt to show birds in an extensive or naturalistically informative setting. There are some exceptions of course: the cockatoos at Hall's Gap, the white-cheeked honeyeaters on wattle, the spiny-cheeked honeyeaters amid gum leaves and so on. But for the most part, the animals seem to him to be themselves landscapes, large and small. We seldom see birds anywhere other than in the planes and spaces which Ray contrives for them — and most often these 'spaces' have more to do with Ray's creative needs than those of the birds. He does not, of course, ever show a creature where in the wild it could not be; neither will he allow it to behave out of character or appear dressed in any way other than in accurately observed colour and pattern.

Gone now is much of the obsessive detail of the early 1970s and, inevitable with any directional change, things are lost, things are gained. The hugely elaborate setpieces such as 'Partridges dusting' (page 25) and 'Blackbird nesting' (page 24), so glorious in their scale and so tightly and fully resolved, give way now to calmer work, usually now less flamboyant, not so immediately impressive, yet showing forces and insights not seen in these earlier works.

Perhaps the decidedly medieval character of The Armoury, his home in Winchelsea, hastened this process. It is entirely natural that in such an environment, the artist's thoughts on painting 'The Gilded Triptych' should finally reach fruition. Parts of this ancient stone house,

RIGHT:
The artist in the vaulted crypt beneath his studio.

the vaulted cellars for example, date from the thirteenth and fourteenth centuries. Huge beams of oak, hundreds of years old, contrast vividly with delicately carved stone corbels. Wide and spacious staircases and large panelled rooms offer solidity and tranquillity.

One might argue that the superb stone archways within The Armoury, the clipped forms of yew topiary within the large gardens, are all to be found, if rather emblematically, within the conceptual form of 'The Gilded Triptych'. It seems, however, to be part of a process in which Ray is increasingly distancing himself from both the tradition of ornithological painting and illustration, as well as from the genre of game animal painting.

Ray is unique among animal artists, with his ability to show us creatures which appear so logical and right — almost as if we had imagined them ourselves — that they hardly look to be painted at all! The distinguished artist and naturalist, Roger Tory Peterson, has defined this edge that Harris-Ching has as 'through-the-eye-realism'. It is probably as close as anyone can get to it.

The Gilded Triptych

'Whereof I had so inly great pleasure
That, as me thought, I surely ravished was Into Paradise . . .'

From *The Flower and the Leaf,*
ANONYMOUS, FIFTEENTH CENTURY.

Without doubt the seeds of this monumental work lie in Harris-Ching's acquisition of the thirteenth century Winchelsea stone house.

Its many beautiful arched stone doorways have clearly impressed themselves on Harris-Ching's overall design for the triptych as, no doubt, has the ancient vaulted crypt beneath the library.

As early as the summer of 1981 drawings for the work began to appear — rough plans, 'maps' of how it might work, cropping up on the margins of drawings or on the backs of panels prepared for other work. By the middle of 1983, while on an extensive field-trip completing the paintings for *New Zealand Birds,* the artist (in New Zealand and 12,000 miles from any medieval buildings) sent the final plans for the frame to the London carvers. The construction and gilding took some seven months, by which time Harris-Ching had returned to England to begin at last the drawings that would bring the triptych to its final form.

Closed, the work is a marriage of blue and gold. Two ducks glide across the front panels, leaving a series of complex patterns in their wake. Typically hard-edged in treatment, the surface remains wonderfully 'wet' in appearance. Both ducks are common European species and their gentle rippling passage entirely supports the painter's wish to establish a calm, undemanding order within the piece for as long as it remains closed.

However, upon opening, the work immediately reveals a startling panorama of some sixty or so birds with a large centre panel of exotically plumaged creatures perching in a tree of violent, Pre-Raphaelite greens.

The species chosen are curious and exotic and exist purely for the artist's pleasure. Even the familiar peacock is not quite as we might suppose — this is the scarcer *green peacock* and it may be seen as pointing the way to the establishment of an order throughout the work, both real and not real. What *is* real are the shapes, the patterns and the colours of all the creatures. They are juxtaposed, however, in a way that is definitely not naturalistic, and yet all are drawn to scale. The importance of scale is established in the reredos panels along the base. These show familiar species — a European blackbird, six house sparrows, a pair of Brewer's blackbirds and a mourning dove — are all painted life size, thereby allowing the birds in the nine main panels above to be rendered smaller than life but all to scale. A small African red-billed hornbill joins company with the sparrows, and the rare New Zealand takahe turns up behind the magnificent head of a golden eagle. Australian cockatoos live here with Asian ducks, a cosmopolitan peregrine falcon soars above the near extinct Japanese ibis while toucans and hornbills appear to be setting up a noisy chatter and clamour directed at buzzards and blue jays on another panel.

LEFT:
Tufted duck front centre left 49.5 x 40.6 cm
(19 ½ x 16")

ABOVE:
North American waders arched top front right
20 x 40.6 cm (7 ¾ x 16")

OVERLEAF (PAGE 34):
Triptych front closed

OVERLEAF (PAGE 35):
Pochard front centre 49.5 x 40.6 cm
(19 ½ x 16")

RIGHT:
The triptych fully opened
oil on panels   111.8 x 215.4 cm   (44 x 84")   1984

36

LEFT:
European buzzard   Harris hawk
Java sparrow   Anna's hummingbird   rhea
black-capped chickadee   blue jay
Centre panel   inside left wing
48.9 x 40 cm   (19¼ x 15¾")

RIGHT:
Golden eagle   cattle egret   sacred ibis
Saker falcon   pink cockatoo   glossy starling
plumed tree-ducks
Centre panel   inside right wing
48.9 x 40 cm   (19¼ x 15¾")

RIGHT:
Green peacock   immature night heron   toucan   Asian hornbill
black and white casqued hornbill   African eagle-owl   white-faced scops owl
king vulture peregrine   Japanese crane   crested screamer
royal spoonbill   ibis   plumed tree-duck   superb starling
Centre panel   70 x 94 cm   (27 ¾ x 37")

ABOVE: House sparrows   Brewer's blackbird (pair)   mourning dove   red-billed hornbill
Centre reredos panel   22 x 94 cm   (8¾ x 37")

ABOVE TOP:
Takahe
Inside right wing   arched top   19 x 40 cm   (7 ½ x 15 ¾")

ABOVE:
Bald eagle and mallard pair
Inside left wing   arched top   19 x 40 cm   (7 ½ x 15 ¾")

RIGHT:
House sparrow and Philippine mallard
Inside left reredos panel   22 x 40 cm   (8 ¾ x 15 ¾")

LEFT:
European blackbird   female sunning
Inside right reredos panel
22 x 40 cm   (8¾ x 15¾")

The last panel to be drawn and fitted, the blackbird sunning herself (page 46), is shown life-size, as are all of the species in the lower reredos panels. Curiously, however, it does not sit in the same 'landscape' as the others. The horizon of wintry trees which links the two other base panels is not present and the resulting unease gives further tension to this already strange work. The closed front appears to show ducks and waders sharing the same body of water, but it couldn't be so — although fine pale reflection lines do extend from the top arched panels into those below to increase the illusion. The lower water panels also look at first to fit, but soon reveal themselves to be drawn quite separately. This same visual device occurs inside — branches make their way across frames from panel to panel but foliage behind them may stop at an edge. Some link up, some do not, but all contribute to the forces present in this fantastic vision.

THE PLATES

In a large cabinet of drawers in his studio, Raymond Harris-Ching houses an extensive collection of toucan and hornbill study-skins and skulls, representing most of the world's species. The skulls look especially beautiful lying in rows, side by side — each an intricate natural sculpture, differing slightly in shape or size or casque ornamentation. Ray shows them to the studio visitor with delight, his fascination with their curious beak structure being as much the reason he returns so often to paint this group of birds as their strikingly bold plumage.

The insides of the hornbills' huge bills are not, as might be supposed, a heavy extension of the skull-bone to hold the great mass together, but are instead composed of the most delicate 'honeycomb', and being filled with air, remain light in weight while still being strong.

The group contains some of the most spectacular of all birds, their often large size and extraordinary beak development (sometimes surmounted by a misshapen casque and patches of bare facial skin) making them quite unforgettable. They are birds of the Old World, occurring in Africa, India, South-East Asia, the Philippines and south to Indonesia, New Guinea and the Solomons. In the New World they are entirely absent and their place as masters of beak development is taken by the toucans, to which, by the way, they are not related.

The nesting habits of some hornbills are as remarkable as their startling appearance. These birds probably pair for life and most will seek out a hole in a tree in which to nest. When about to lay, the female will climb into the nest hole and allow the male to plaster up the entrance behind her. A mud mixture is used and usually the soon-to-be-entombed partner contributes to the walling-in from her side of the opening. Once set, the mixture hardens to become an exceptionally effective barrier against predators — monkeys especially — and when everything is finished, the only aperture remaining is a slit, just wide enough to allow the female to stick out her beak. With this opening as her only means of contact with the outside world, she is confined to these cramped quarters for at least six weeks although, depending on the species, the period of imprisonment may last for twice that time! Throughout these weeks her partner dutifully brings food to the nest and when finally she does break free, dirty and bedraggled, she is stiff and out of condition and barely able to fly. The break for freedom usually occurs when the chicks are about half grown, by which time the wall has become so hard that it is broken down only with considerable effort. After the mother leaves, the young may repair the breached wall, sealing themselves back in, to rely on the parent birds bringing food until the time is right for their own release.

Black and white casqued hornbills inhabit much of equatorial Africa from Kenya, Tanzania and Uganda in the east to the Cameroons and the Ivory Coast in the west, where in some parts of their range they are quite common.

RIGHT:
Black and white casqued hornbill   *Bycanistes subcylindricus*
oil on panel   46 x 36 cm   (18¼ x 14")   (detail)   1984

OVERLEAF LEFT:
Black and white casqued hornbill   *B. subcylindricus*   head study
oil on panel   30 x 20 cm   (12 x 8")   1984

OVERLEAF CENTRE:
Black and white casqued hornbill   *B. subcylindricus*
pencil   38 x 26 cm   (15 x 10¼")   1984

OVERLEAF RIGHT:
Black and white casqued hornbill   (preening and stretching)   *B. subcylindricus*
watercolour   74 x 53 cm   (29 x 21")   undated

Harris-Ching feels there isn't too much difference between drawing medium-sized 'wild' cats (such as the serval painted here) and many domestic tabbies; indeed, he is intrigued, he says, by just how similar their expressions and movements often are, even though the one is indulged by us, while the other makes its own way in a much less forgiving world.

Servals are often described in rather indifferent terms — their leggy build and comparatively short tails offer unusual proportions and the sandy colouring is not especially remarkable. Yet as Harris-Ching shows us here, this is a subtly beautiful animal: the coat gently spotted, the face small and intelligent, and the slightly ungainly nature of the creature's build can have a unity and grace about it not, perhaps, at first obvious.

They are one of the more common species of cats found in Africa and, indeed, their range covers much of the continent.

LEFT:
Serval   *Felis serval*
oil   58 x 46 cm   (23 x 18")   arched top   1979

RIGHT:
Serval   *F. serval*   head study
oil on canvas   30 x 41 cm   (12 x 16")   1980

Dark-eyed falcons are an especially interesting problem for the painter in that, most usually, determined and fierce behaviour is best depicted by the bright yellowy eyes of, say, a lion or a sparrowhawk. The desert falcons are as swift and dangerous as can be, but their large deep eyes seem, to the painter at least, to mask this ferocity.

Several species of falcon — the lanner, the lagger, the prairie and the saker — all show a preference for arid or semi-arid country, and in the various parts of the world that they inhabit each is usually considered the ecological counterpart of the others. The darker bird painted on the ground at the top of the studies is an immature lanner and the bird figured at the base is a cross between a peregrine and barbary falcon.

The saker has for hundreds of years been a favourite of Arab falconers who admire its hardy nature and indiscriminate taste, which make it ideally suited to hunting in desert conditions.

Lanners are the typical desert falcons of Africa. Indeed, they are the most common of the larger African falcons, inhabiting savannah and semi-desert areas throughout the continent, and reaching their greatest abundance south of the Sahara. In addition to their African distribution, lanners can be found in scattered populations throughout the Middle East and even parts of southern Europe.

Like the saker, lanners enjoy a varied diet (mammals, birds, reptiles and even insects) but small birds make up the largest proportion of their food. As might be expected, the lanner takes prey in the air rather more often than does its relative, the saker.

The population and range of sakers is, however, in decline and fears for the species are expressed from time to time. Similarly, the range of the lanner is contracting, particularly in Europe, although neither looks to be under any immediate threat.

LEFT:
Saker   *Falco cherrug*
oil on panel   53.3 x 39.4 cm   (21 x 15½")   1975

RIGHT:
Desert falcon studies   *F. peregrinoids*
oil   45.7 x 35.6 cm   (18 x 14")   1983

This small picture, hardly larger than reproduced here, is more a drawing in oils than a developed painting. It is loosely sketched, in very thin colours, the brush used as a pencil and no overpainting has been troubled with in such a small and necessarily very quick, study.

LEFT:
Caracal   *Felis caracal*   oil on panel   24.1 x 35.6 cm   (9½ x 14")   1983

Nearly all of Ray's studies of these large cats have been drawn from captive animals in various European collections and I imagine that perhaps the spirit of these works does reflect that.

On the plains of Africa, without serious enemy or rival, the lion carries all the trappings of power and ferocity, its great size and musculature one of the most formidable and imposing sights in the animal kingdom.

With such physical superiority, the lion faces few restrictions to its diet — zebra, wildebeest and buffalo are among species commonly secured.

Although that other great cat, the tiger, is a largely silent animal, lions are very much the opposite and their roar, a truly inspiring sound, is celebrated widely in the writings of those who have spent time in Africa. The volume of noise produced in a full-throated blast can be heard from a long way off and is likely to leave a powerful impression! Roars are not the only sounds lions make — apparently animals disturbed in cover emit low warning growls which, when hunched over prey, change to a booming, more aggressive sound.

Apart from a remnant population of Asiatic lions living in the Gir Forest, India, lions are now confined to Africa. In historical times their range was much wider and indeed, until quite recently, they could be found across much of India and westward through Iran to parts of the Middle East. Now, even in Africa, their range continues to be reduced as they are driven back into wilder, remoter regions or into the great game parks.

ABOVE:
Lion   *Panthera leo*
oil   23.5 x 35.6 cm   (9¼ x 14")   1981

ABOVE LEFT:
Lion   *P. leo*
study   oil   26 x 35.6 cm   (10¼ x 14")   1980

RIGHT:
Lion   adult male   *P. leo*   head study
oil   reproduced actual size   1983

Chimpanzees may live to fifty years or more in the forests and woodland savannah that form their natural habitat in central, east and west Africa. They are the smallest of the great apes and certainly one of the most familiar. Both males and females have coats of longish black hair (the young have a white tuft on their rumps) and, interestingly, it is the females who are most prone to early baldness!

Their short thumbs, yet long fingers, make precision gripping impossible, but chimps are able to use a great variety of objects as tools — sticks for poking into trees or termite holes, for instance.

Their excitable, highly social behaviour is well documented and groups may grow to include seventy to eighty individuals. Chimps have highly expressive faces and employ a great series of highly pitched barks and hoots to communicate a wide variety of messages. Tensions in a group are often lessened by social grooming — adult males may groom each other — or grooming parties of ten or so may be formed by, perhaps, a mother with several offspring.

ABOVE RIGHT:
Common chimpanzee   *Pan troglodytes*
oil on canvas   39.4 x 52 cm   (15½ x 20½")
1980

RIGHT:
Crested porcupine   *Hystrix cristata*
oil   36.2 x 47 cm   (14¼ x 18½")   1980

FAR RIGHT:
Black bear
oil on panel   29.2 x 22.2 cm   (11½ x 8¾")
1984

This is, quite simply, the artist's favourite bird to paint and probably figures in more of his paintings than any other.

Harris-Ching urges us to take time to look at these two perfect things, searching here for fallen seeds or some such in muddy farm tracks. These familiar birds can, of course, be seen in most towns or cities where this opportunistic species represents much that most intrigues the artist about birds. Indeed, for many town dwellers the world over *Passer domesticus* is one of the few birds they may regularly see — the street pigeon in this respect, being the only serious rival. It may be that the sparrow is familiar to more people in more parts of the world than any other kind of bird, and the key to its remarkable spread must surely be the sparrow's adaptation to cope with environments created by modern man.

Sparrows are highly social birds, as well as somewhat promiscuous — their fights and noisy courtships have long been the subject of human interest and their squabblings and constant chatter may offer welcome colour to the daily drudge of many town dwellers.

Sparrows remain, to most people, simply rather charming small birds, responding to humans in very definite ways, allowing at times quite close approach, yet in the end staying wild and wary. They might seem, at some passing glance, to be drably dressed, yet on close inspection the plumage, especially that of the male, is marvellously attractive with the subtlest variety of markings.

LEFT:
House sparrow   pair   *Passer domesticus*   oil on panel   59.7 x 42 cm
(23 ½ x 16 ½ ")   1981

On the occasion that the artist first saw a shrew, he heard first a screech of high pitched fury from the open base of an outside drainpipe, and discovered this tiny animal trapped and cornered, no doubt by some domestic cat, and furious at the indignity of it all. Harris-Ching was fascinated by such rage and aggression from a creature, in life, only the size of the watercolour study reproduced on this page!

There's no doubt that the common shrew, at around 50 millimetres long (excluding the tail), is a pugnacious, highly aggressive little insectivore which burns so much energy it needs to be almost continually feeding. So aggressive are shrews that if two are imprisoned together, it will not be long before the stronger kills the weaker.

However, the secretive nature of shrews makes them difficult to observe and they are, in consequence, more often found dead (usually the victim of a house cat) than seen alive. In fact, cats regularly kill shrews and do not, apparently, eat them because of a strong odour given off; this scent doesn't, however, seem to deter owls, who most certainly include them in their diets.

Superficially, shrews show a considerable resemblance to mice, but when looked at closely, the differences are quite pronounced and unmistakable — the long, pointed snout of the shrews and the protruding, sickle shape of the first pair of front teeth (in common shrews, stained reddish brown), clearly distinguishing them from other rodents.

Common shrews prefer woodlands, where they may pass so carefully beneath the blanket of fallen leaves as to go completely unnoticed. They also show a liking for life in fields, either rough grassland or cultivated farmland, and can be found living close to marshes or in duneland areas.

There are a large number of shrew species, found both in the Old and New Worlds; the one painted here is a native of Europe, Asia and North America.

ABOVE:
Common shrew   *Sorex araneus*
watercolour   undated

RIGHT:
Common shrew   sunning   *S. araneus*
gouache   undated

LEFT:
European robin   *Erithacus rubecula*
watercolour (detail)
61 x 43.2 cm   (24 x 17")   1978

The painter has said that he wanted to contrast these forgotten, long since dried-up paint tins in an unused corner of a shed with the beginning of things, represented by a robin sitting low on her eggs and conveying the expectancy of new life and of cycles repeated.

This dry-brush watercolour is one of a group of elaborate 'set pieces' from the early and mid 1970s, all of which show familiar birds in a controlled and highly resolved setting, and always drawn in their natural size. However, unlike some earlier studies where each nail, tin box, brick and cobweb is finely rendered and completely resolved, this robin represents the beginnings of a looser, less nervous style, that was to develop and eventually dominate Harris-Ching's work into the early 1980s.

Robins choose to nest in dark, sheltered spots among woodland undergrowth, or in holes or cavities close to the ground, perhaps in the roots of a tree. In parts of Europe (most typically in Britain), robins have moved out from more traditional habitats to take advantage of the opportunities provided by parks and gardens where any recess or hole in a building is likely to be used. The nest itself is formed by the female into the shape of a rather bulky cup from leaves, grasses and mosses, and is given a lining of rootlets, hair and occasionally feathers. Depending on geographical location, robins may breed at any time between March and June, a typical clutch consisting of five or six cream-coloured eggs, marked with brown or lavender. As she takes responsibility for nest building, so the female undertakes the task of sitting on the eggs; the male doesn't, however, escape all responsibility for throughout the incubation period he keeps his mate supplied with food and even after the young have hatched continues to tend them.

Robins are highly territorial and when any assumed rights are encroached upon, are fiercely aggressive towards other robins. Both sexes, by the way, look the same.

ABOVE: Female mallard *Anas platyrhynchos* 41.9 x 35.6 cm (16½ x 14") 1981

ABOVE: Domestic duck   oil on panel   25.4 x 33 cm   (10 x 13")   1985

RIGHT: Young swans   oil on panel   1986

'I can't think of any kingfishers that I might have painted in a size other than life-size, for it has always seemed to me that their energetic shape, and usually brilliant hues, entirely relate to their scale. Sparrows strike me as the same – everything about them demands they be painted precisely in their natural size.'

The common kingfisher of Europe, Asia and Africa is a truly jewel-like bird, and over much of its European range it is one of the very few really brightly coloured species seen, so that when glimpsed, even fleetingly, it is unlikely to be confused with any other bird.

Although kingfishers can be found close to many kinds of running or still fresh water, their preference is for narrow streams or small and quiet lakes or ponds, and generally, they avoid wider stretches of open water or broader rivers. Food consists mainly of small fish, but they will readily take aquatic insects, frogs, tadpoles and other amphibians.

In the European breeding season from April to August, kingfishers nest in holes, usually made in banks by an adult pair flying vigorously back and forth until a tunnel has been excavated (perhaps a metre long), which they eventually line with small fishbones.

FAR LEFT:
European kingfisher   *Alcedo atthis*
oil on panel   43.2 x 33 cm   (17 x 13")   1976

LEFT:
European kingfisher   *A. atthis*   diving
oil on panel   43.2 x 33 cm   (17 x 13")   1976

RIGHT:
European kingfisher   *A. atthis*   at nest bank
watercolour   68.6 x 53.3 cm   (27 x 21")   1975

Small owls can be found in many parts of the world and in all sorts of environments, but those known specifically as 'little owls' are restricted to the northern hemisphere of the Old World.

There are three species — the spotted little owl, the forest little owl and the little owl itself, which is by far the most widespread and familiar, and in Harris-Ching's painting is represented by a fledgling bird barely out of the nest.

Little owls favour open or lightly forested country, although the species is not particularly daunted by the presence of humans and is often found in parklands and cultivated areas. These owls are far from strictly nocturnal and are quite likely to be spotted during the day hunting from fence posts, diving to secure insects — beetles and grasshoppers mostly — but small rodents, frogs, lizards and songbirds are also taken. The birds run surprisingly rapidly — indeed, their close relative, the burrowing owl of the New World, lives almost exclusively on the ground.

RIGHT:
Little owl *Athene noctua*
watercolour and gouache   53.3 x 40.6 cm
(21 x 16")   1975

This beautiful creature, killed by oil polluting its feathers, was brought to the artist one Christmas Day. Ray recounts that it cost him a cold Christmas dinner and some grumpy looks from his family for spending the day yet again in the studio, but it had to be painted there and then, for it could be kept fresh only a day or two in the studio.

He chose not to show the tragically oiled breast, but instead, painted the elegant 'Art Deco' shapes and colours of its back which, along with its tiny pointed wings, gives the bird such a distinctive appearance.

These sleek razorbills with their grotesque, yet strangely streamlined beaks belong to the family Alcidae, a group of more than twenty species which go under a variety of names: auks, murries, dovekies, guillemots, puffins etc. — all of which are well adapted to life in the cold seas.

The Alcidae are the ecological counterparts, in northern waters, of the penguins found in southern seas. Although these two groups bear no close relationship to each other, in appearance they are superficially similar and even in colouring — largely black and white — they are comparable. In one obvious way, however, they are quite dissimilar: whereas all penguin species have lost the power of flight (so as to develop their wings for maximum efficiency in water) no living Alcid is flightless.

Of all recent members of the Alcidae family, only the celebrated great auk had evolved so completely to a watery existence that it was unable to fly. This remarkable bird, although twice as large as the razorbill, bore, nonetheless, a most striking resemblance to its smaller relative. Although once very numerous in the polar seas great auks were severely persecuted by seafarers and others with whom they came in contact, particularly when waddling about helplessly on shore. Our last recorded encounter with the species came in June 1844 when a pair were killed on the island of Eldey off the Icelandic coast. Since then it has generally been considered extinct.

Its smaller relative has, however, fared better and razorbills come ashore to breed in their hundreds of thousands on the coasts that fringe both sides of the North Atlantic.

They make their homes on the ledges and in the cracks of high sea-cliffs or stacks, preferring islands isolated from the mainland. Like other Alcids, razorbills breed in great colonies, often in company with many thousands of other seabirds. Just a single egg is laid, usually in a fissure on the bare rock, and the eggs of razorbills vary greatly in colour — they may be bluish or greenish, white or showing a yellow tinge — but usually, all are blotched and spotted with brown.

LEFT:
Razorbill *Alca torda* watercolour 43.2 x 34.3 cm (17 x 13½") 1975

By the late 1970s, Harris-Ching had perfect control over painted water. He can choose to show it as ever more complex patterns or in a single, often startling colour. The waterfowl he depicts are almost invariably quite common species whose very familiarity exactly suits the artist's purpose.

LEFT:
Tufted duck *Aythya fuligula*
oil on panel 43.2 x 35.6 cm (17 x 14")
undated

ABOVE:
Mandarin duck female *Aix galericulata*
oil on panel 35.6 x 22.9 cm (14 x 9")
undated

RIGHT:
Pochard eclipse bird *Aythya ferina*
oil on panel 48.3 x 35.6 cm (19 x 14")
undated

A series of life-sized watercolour studies of bees made at a time when the artist needed to show in a painting a pair of young owls disturbing a hive of honey bees. The bees in the sketch are *Bombus locorum* and were not those used in the final painting, but the drawing is clearly carried out with as much interest and attention as the production of the eventual painting.

ABOVE LEFT:
Nest of goldcrest   *Regulus regulus*   watercolour and bodycolour   25.4 x 20.3 cm   (10 x 8")   1974

ABOVE RIGHT:
Nest   watercolour and bodycolour   38.1 x 25.4 cm   (15 x 10")   1974

RIGHT:
Bees   *Bombus locorum*   watercolour   22.2 x 26.7 cm   (8¾ x 10½")   1975

The fledgling song thrush in this watercolour study leaps at an insect off the page, unseen by us, and Ray may have allowed himself to become more than just a little 'Audubonesque'. Its actions are exaggerated but perhaps, at times and for some paintings, this may be no bad thing. His study of the cock house sparrow feeding its newly fledged young is quite the opposite — straightforward and naturalistically shown.

ABOVE:
House sparrow   *Passer domesticus*   adult male feeding young   oil
49.5 x 36.8 cm   (19½ x 14½")   1984

RIGHT:
Song thrush   fledgling bird   *Turdus philomelos*   watercolour   detail
66 x 53.3 cm   (26 x 21")   1974

LEFT:
Grey partridge   *Perdix perdix*
watercolour and pencil   33 x 25.4 cm
(13 x 10")   1972

ABOVE LEFT:
Song thrush   *Turdus philomelos*
watercolour   25.4 x 20.3 cm   (10 x 8")   1974

ABOVE CENTRE:
Long-tailed tit   *Aegithalos caudatus*
watercolour   22.9 x 15.2 cm   (9 x 6")
undated

ABOVE FAR RIGHT:
Common moorhen (immature)   *Gallinula chloropus*
watercolour   63.5 x 45.7 cm   (25 x 18")
1972

BELOW RIGHT:
Starling   *Sturnus vulgaris*
watercolour   21.6 x 15.9 cm   (8½ x 6¼")
1973

BELOW CENTRE:
Redwing   *Turdus iliacus*
watercolour   22.9 x 17.8 cm   (9 x 7")   1974

BELOW FAR RIGHT:
Wren   *Troglodytes troglodytes*
watercolour   life size   undated

LEFT:
Brambles (pre-study for 'Wrens') watercolour 41.9 x 35.6 cm (16½ x 14") 1974

ABOVE:
Pheasant (nesting) *Phasianus colchicus* watercolour 69.9. x 52.7 cm (27½ x 20¾") 1978

ABOVE RIGHT:
Partridge *Perdix perdix* acrylic on paper 73 x 55 cm (28¾ x 21⅝") 1979

The variety and splendour of the patterns and colouring among pheasant species finds its most extreme development in the peacock — perhaps the most outrageously dressed of all the world's birds. The male common pheasant, although less beautifully marked has, nonetheless, a rich yet subtle patterning that is remarkably attractive. The female, too, is a beautiful creature with her combination of delicate browns designed to make her unobtrusive — except to the eye of the painter! In these large watercolours, both pheasant and partridge are shown lifesize, hidden away in the dense borders of a hedgerow. Harris-Ching's ability to suggest the space between, behind and around the leaves he paints is one of his most powerful illusions.

RIGHT:
Sedge warbler   *Acrocephalus schoenobaenus*
watercolour   73.3 x 55.3 cm
(28 ½ x 21 ¾")   1978

FAR RIGHT:
Grasses   watercolour   45.7 x 53.3 cm
(18 x 21")   1978

Painted in high summer in the grounds of an old school in Kent, this watercolour might be argued as too sentimental and perhaps it is — the tap slowly drips, summer flies buzz about and the wrens wait. But it is just such a 'sentimental' scene that the observant walker is likely to stumble upon when ambling quietly through the English countryside.

In Europe there is just the single wren species, but in the Americas there are about sixty species. There the wren becomes the 'winter wren' to avoid confusion.

Quite why only one species has been able to cross the Bering Strait and colonise Eurasia is not immediately obvious, but what can be said is that this colonisation is not particularly recent; more than twenty distinct races of wren have been described from the Old World and subfossil remains of wrens have been found in European deposits of Pleistocene age.

The range of the wren shows several other apparent anomalies. It has a stronghold in Europe, where it occurs almost everywhere except in the more northerly parts of Scandinavia. In Iceland, Asia Minor and even parts of North Africa it is also present, and the species has a scattered distribution in central Asia. It is also widespread in eastern China and Manchuria and is also found in Japan. In North America the winter wren's range is confined to the north where it breeds across the whole of the southern half of Canada and although its range south does extend deep into the United States, this is mostly only in mountainous areas. It seems likely that interspecific competition with other wren species prevents the winter wren from occupying the more southerly environments that its counterparts in Eurasia are able to exploit.

Typically, wrens are found in dark, damp places, in which they can be seen scuttling about in their unmistakable mouselike fashion.

Wrens will nest in almost any cavity but usually close to ground level, and it is the males who build the outer shell into a stout, domed construction of moss, grasses and leaves. Usually, several nests are built to allow the female to select the one she likes best. After her choice is made, she completes the structure with a careful lining of feathers and other soft materials. The eggs laid are whitish with some very fine black or brown speckling at the larger end, and are incubated by the female without help from her partner, although he does assist with feeding duties.

LEFT:
Wren   *Troglodytes troglodytes*   watercolour   73.7 x 52.1 cm   (29 x 20½")   undated

RIGHT:
Winter wrens   *Troglodytes troglodytes*   watercolour   71.1 x 53.3 cm   (28 x 21")   detail   1971

ABOVE:
European buzzard   *Buteo buteo*   headstudy   oil on panel   16.9 x 24.1 cm   (6 ⅝ x 9 ½")   1985

RIGHT:
European buzzard   *B. buteo*   oil on panel   47 x 34.9 cm   (18 ½ x 13 ¾")
1984

LEFT:
European sparrowhawk   *Accipiter nisus*
oil on chalk ground   60.7 x 48.3 cm   (24 x 19")
1976

Several weeks were spent preparing the perfectly smooth, fine, gypsum chalk ground as a base on which to paint this study of a large female sparrowhawk, sunning and dusting. It is the only occasion of which I am aware of the painter using such a surface — a possible drawback might be the weight on the wall of the final painting with its base of inch-thick wood panels!

The artist called early one evening on a friend who cares for injured wild animals and was shown a young barn owl, brought in just that day, dishevelled and quite frightened. Their presence further frightened the bird which immediately flipped on to its back, talons raised, snapping its beak and all the while hissing like air escaping from a tyre. Ray quickly retreated to leave the bird in peace, but never forgot the shapes and sounds that it made. Here, he has contrived to make it you, viewer of the painting, who frightens the cornered bird. And so that the presence of a human is suggested (and not that, say, of a fox or some other possible predator), he has shown the owl against stones at the bottom of a garden — a domestic rather than wild setting.

In the pitch dark the barn owl is able to detect its prey by sound alone if necessary and in flight can be entirely silent, leaving the rodent or other small creature on which it is preying, completely unaware of its approach. Usually, they are nocturnal but they can, nonetheless, be seen from time to time before dark and certainly, when driving at dusk, its ghostly white form is often illuminated in motor car headlights.

Barn owls show no great dislike for the presence of humans and disused farm buildings have become particularly favoured haunts. The species is distributed across much of both the Old and New Worlds, where the bird is able to adapt to many differing types of habitat; its preference, however, seems to be for lightly wooded land close to areas of open country.

ABOVE:
Barn owl   *Tyto alba*
watercolour   71.8 x 52.1 cm   (28¼ x 20½")
1979

ABOVE:
European hare (sunning) *Lepus europaeus*
oil   45.7 x 34.3 cm   (18 x 13½")   1978

RIGHT:
Golden eagle   *Aquila chrysaëtos*
oil on panel   36.8 x 49.5 cm   (14½ x 19½")   1983

The American kestrel — often called 'sparrowhawk' — is, in fact, a small falcon (the second smallest in its genus) and considerably smaller, for example, than its Old World relative, the European kestrel. Although unmistakably different in colour, patterning and size, the two species are in several respects similar: both show the same habit of hovering in wind over open country to watch for any movement on the ground below and both are able to tolerate the close presence of humans, which is probably why they are among the most commonly seen of all birds of prey.

BELOW:
American kestrel   *Falco sparverius*
oil   33 x 25.4 cm   (13 x 10")   undated

ABOVE:
American kestrel   male bird   *F. sparverius*
oil   33.7 x 25.4 cm   (13¼ x 10")   undated

LEFT:
Peregrine   *F. peregrinus*
pencil   50.8 x 35.6 cm   (20 x 14")   undated

In Virginia, where this watercolour was painted, mourning doves will usually have already moved south by the time of the first snows. The idea of showing them in a landscape of light snow will have appealed to the artist, as much as anything, just because of its unexpectedness.

The birds are named for their sad, drawn-out, repetitious cooing — a call that on still mornings in early summer often greets the first light of dawn.

In appearance the species shows some similarity to its extinct relative, the passenger pigeon, although it is rather smaller and less strikingly coloured. Once, passenger pigeons could be counted in their millions, but now it is the mourning dove that is the most common and widespread of all indigenous North American pigeons.

Typically birds of open country, mourning doves use small stands of woodland for shelter and nesting, and generally like to be close to water so that they may drink and bathe in both the morning and evening.

LEFT AND ABOVE:
Mourning doves *Zenaidura macroura*
watercolour   71.1 x 54.6 cm   (28 x 21½")   1980

Bald eagles are no longer found over much of their former range, but in those wild places where they can still be seen these large birds, with their startling snow-white heads, look every bit equal to their status as the national emblem of the United States. Yet despite such impressive appearance, its voice, surprisingly, is a rather weak, croaky squeak, which at times sounds not unlike that of a gull.

Its great size and power enables the bald eagle to take large mammals and birds, but the species will readily resort to creatures that may seem to us beneath its dignity — frogs, for example, along with some other amphibians have been recorded as occasional items of diet.

The nests of bald eagles are, however, truly spectacular, though noteworthy more for their great size rather than for any particular aesthetic effect. A mated pair will build a nest each year, and what makes their creation remarkable is that each new structure is built on top of the old one, resulting over a period of years in the nest often becoming so vast and heavy as to kill the tree in which it is placed. Trees, however, are not the only nesting sites chosen — rocky outcrops and crags may sometimes be used, where nests have been measured that are 3–4 metres high and 2–3 metres across.

RIGHT:
Bald eagle   *Haliaeetus leucocephalus*
pencil studies   53.3 x 40.6 cm   (21 x 16")
undated

FAR RIGHT:
Bald eagle   *H. leucocephalus*
oil   63.5 x 45.7 cm   (25 x 18")   undated

ABOVE:
Kittiwake   *Rissa tridactyla*   oil   81.3 x 86.4 cm   (32 x 34")   undated

RIGHT:
Polar bear   *Thalarctos maritimus*   oil   30.5 x 40.6 cm   (12 x 16")   1979

An arched top was introduced to the frame for the first of these heron studies, not so much because the spirit of the bird demanded it, but because the study was painted so thinly, so clearly and transparently, as to reflect (although without the bright colours), the nineteenth century Pre-Raphaelite aspirations which so appeal to the artist.

Black-crowned night herons are most active during the hours of darkness and although they can be seen during the day the species stays generally quiet and still, hidden in heavy cover, to emerge only at dusk when it might be noticed by its guttural and rather eerie croaks as it passes overhead.

Night herons favour shallow water where they catch small fish and amphibians by patiently standing perfectly still until some unwary prey presents itself.

LEFT:
Anna's hummingbird females   *Calypte anna*
oil on panel   33 x 49.5 cm   (13 x 19¼")
1980

ABOVE RIGHT:
Black-crowned night heron   *Nycticorax nycticorax*
oil on panel   25.4 x 39.4 cm   (10 x 15½")
arched top   1984

RIGHT:
Black-crowned night heron   *N. nycticorax*
oil on panel   24.1 x 30.5 cm   (9½ x 12")
undated

These North American waterfowl form part of a continuing series of 'birds in water' that began with a pochard on a farm pond in England. The swan, the largest of these birds in life, is depicted in the smallest painting; indeed, the work is shown here about actual size.

BELOW:
Wood duck   adult male   *Aix sponsa*
oil   52.1 x 40.6 cm   (20½ x 16")   undated

RIGHT:
Whistling swan   *Cygnus olor*
oil   30.5 x 22.9 cm   (12 x 9")   undated

ABOVE:
American widgeon   *Anas americana*
oil   38.1 x 30.5 cm   (15 x 12")   undated

RIGHT:
Canvasback   adult male   *Aythya valisineria*
oil   45.7 x 35.6 cm   (18 x 14")   1980

Pochards were among the first waterfowl painted by Harris-Ching, whose interest lay as much with the patterns of water as with the bird itself. The artist has rarely treated water as something simply to hold the bird up just to allow its fine plumage to be painted, but increasingly the emphasis has shifted to where, now, in some paintings, the bird is used just to disturb the water's surface and to make patterns that are fascinating to paint.

Diving ducks form a group of medium-sized waterfowl showing a marked preference for fresh water, all characterised by short, rather heavy bodies, large feet (each with distinctive flaps on the hind toes) and by stumpy legs positioned far apart and well back. This unusual positioning of the legs — very noticeable when compared with most other ducks — is a splendid adaptation to its aquatic mode of existence, but one of its consequences is the stiff, ungainly waddle that characterises its walk and may well be why, almost always, Harris-Ching elects to show it in the water! The majority of diving ducks are concentrated in the Northern Hemisphere where, as a rule, they are very gregarious, particularly in winter and, of course, when forming huge flocks prior to migration.

Within the group there are a number of very familiar species. In Europe, one of the most widespread is the common pochard, which in North America is replaced by two close relatives — the canvasback and the redhead.

LEFT:
Redhead   *Aythya americana*
oil   54.6 x 43.8 cm   (21½ x 17¼")   1981

RIGHT:
European pochard   *A. ferina*
oil   55.9 x 45.7 cm   (22 x 18")   1981

In this small study of a partridge sunning in low afternoon light, Harris-Ching has returned to a device that he has valued from his earliest paintings. Repeatedly he has used the simple form of a single creature (most often a bird, but mammals are used) pictured in a straightforward manner, more or less in the centre of a plane, on a surface most usually of soil and necessarily of no particular distinction. Fallen leaves or muddy tracks will do for a pair of house sparrows; a hare sunning itself on recently turned turf; a sparse falling of delicately coloured gum leaves lie with a great red kangaroo; the frightened barn owl flipped on to its back amid garden rockery; a sparrowhawk dustbathing at the base of a clay bank — all employ the same simple yet startling device.

LEFT:
Purple finch   *Carpodacus purpureus*
oil   30.5 x 22.9 cm   (12 x 9")   undated

RIGHT:
Grey partridge   *Perdix perdix*
oil on panel   50.8 x 38.1 cm   (20 x 15")   1982

ABOVE: Domestic rabbits   oil   22.9 x 30.5 cm   (9 x 12")   1979

ABOVE: Domestic fowl and chicks   oil on panel   21.6 x 30.5 cm   (8½ x 12")   undated

Otters, wherever they are found, arouse considerable human curiosity and their habits and personalities have formed the basis of several books. Harris-Ching's interest in these animals, however, has centred on the effects of water on their fur and most especially, the way that light reflects on this surface as they swim. The ripples of water and the furrows of fur look as one — and for the painter the otter might hardly be there, so much does it move and look like water itself.

ABOVE LEFT:
Sea lion
oil on panel   22.9 x 31.1 cm   (9 x 12¼")   1984

LEFT:
Sea lions
oil on panel   22.9 x 31.1 cm   (9 x 12¼")   1982

RIGHT:
Otter
oil on panel   23.5 x 30.5 cm   (9¼ x 12")   1984

ABOVE:
Macaque   female
oil on panel   32.4 x 25.4 cm   (12¾ x 10")   1984

LEFT:
Macaque
pencil   28.6 x 22.9 cm   (11¼ x 9")   1984

ABOVE:
Macaque young male
oil on panel 26.7 x 33 cm (10½ x 13") 1984

There are some sixteen species of macaque, varied enough to succed in environments as diverse as mountain forests and mangrove swamps. All are medium-sized, sturdy monkeys, at home both on the ground or in trees where, depending on the nature of the habitat they occupy, they may live in large or small groups.

Within the genus *Macaca* are several quite familiar species including the Japanese macaque which swims in the sea (where it washes sweet potatoes before eating them), and the celebrated Barbary ape of Gibraltar.

The nilgai's impressive size and resigned demeanor gives the creature an air of curious improbability. The bulky dignity of these animals, perceived neither quite as antelope nor cattle, has repeatedly attracted the artist to this species.

ABOVE:
Nilgai   adult female   *Bucelaphus tragocamelus*
oil on canvas   25.4 x 35.6 cm   (10 x 14")   1979

LEFT:
Nilgai   fawn   *B. tragocamelus*
oil   30.5 x 35.6 cm   (12 x 14")   undated

RIGHT:
Nilgai   adult male   *B. tragocamelus*
oil on panel 25.7 x 32.7 cm   (10⅛ x 12⅞")   1984

These great cats have now been reduced to alarmingly small numbers and Ray's interest in drawing them specifically stemmed from a commission to prepare part of the design for sculptured panels to appear on a silver rose bowl, cast to promote the World Wildlife Fund. Perhaps such a large exotic cat would not otherwise have attracted his attention, but over a period of several weeks he made a number of drawings and small paintings, some of which are reproduced here and remain his only studies of this animal.

With its great power and ferocity, stunningly beautiful appearance, solitary nature and propensity for man-eating, the tiger evokes both fear and admiration in almost equal degrees, and leaves us in no doubt that it is among the most imposing of all terrestrial animals.

Essentially, they are night creatures — usually laying up through the day, hidden by long grasses or forest thicket. In fact, tigers show a dislike for the heat of the day, as much as possible sheltering from strong sun and even taking to water in order to keep cool. This fondness for bathing might seem surprising but tigers may swim for miles from river island to river island in search of prey, and have even been known to cross narrow arms of the sea.

LEFT:
Tiger   *Panthera tigris*
oil on panel   27.9 x 22.9 cm   (11 x 9")   1975

RIGHT:
Tiger   *P. tigris*
oil on panel   30.5 x 22.9 cm   (12 x 9")   1975

PAGE 126 (TOP):
Tiger   P. tigris   watercolour   48.3 x 68.6 cm   (19 x 27")   1975

PAGE 126 (BOTTOM):
Tiger   P. tigris   watercolour study   43.2 x 58.4 cm   (17 x 23")   1975

PAGE 127:
Tiger   P. tigris   oil on panel   21.6 x 35.6 cm   (8½ x 14")   1980

RIGHT:
Tiger   P. tigris   oil on panel   20.3 x 30.5 cm   (8 x 12")   1980

It may be difficult to appreciate, when seen against the backdrop of a zoo or game park, that the spectacularly beautiful coat of the tiger is really such an efficient camouflage. Only when we encounter it in its natural habitat do we understand why what seems to us to be striking decoration is, in fact, an excellent agent of disguise. The violent contrasts between the orange and black stripes harmonise with the patterning of light and shade as the animal stalks through broad blades of grass and clumps of reed stems.

Although tigers living in the wild can still be counted in their thousands, the species must, nonetheless, be considered seriously threatened. For an animal whose interests at times so obviously conflict with those of humans, the tiger's future as a free, wild creature is seriously in doubt.

RIGHT:
Common squirrel monkey *Saimiri sciureus*
oil on panel   27.9 x 35.6 cm   (11 x 14")
(arched top)   1984

It is in the 'middle levels' of the tropical rain forests of South America that squirrel monkeys spend most of their day, although from time to time they move to the upper canopy and to the forest's floor, searching out their food of insects and fruits.

These are small monkeys, their head and body hardly 30 centimetres long, with a tail perhaps just a little longer. In this little oil study Harris-Ching has precisely defined the essence of their delicate, distinctive form.

Like the squirrel monkey, the aptly-named spectacled owl is an inhabitant of South American rain forests where its range extends over a vast area, from southern Mexico in the north to northern Argentina in the south. Despite such extensive distribution, remarkably little is known of the species; presumably, the hostile nature of the terrain it occupies accounts for much of this lack of information.

Although medium-sized, these owls are nonetheless able to take surprisingly large prey but, as might be expected, small mammals constitute the most important part of what is eaten. The birds vary their diet to include insects (substantially-sized caterpillars are quite welcome), and bats and birds. This owl doesn't appear to be strictly nocturnal, but it probably remains fairly inactive during most of the day.

Apparently, the species nests in holes in trees but little information about its breeding habits is on record. The physical appearance of the young bird is, however, well enough known and, if anything, may be more striking than its parents — its plumage is a startling white, with the facial disc a sombre black in marked contrast to the rest of the feathering and affording a most dramatic surrounding for the bright yellow eyes.

ABOVE: Spectacled owl   *Pulsatrix perspicillata*
oil   48.3 x 35.6 cm   (19 x 14")   undated

Water presents the same problems and possibilities to the artist whether he depicts herons in Asia, cormorants in Africa or waterfowl in the Americas — seen as deep greens or pale greens, seen broken by waves or smooth as glass, seen murky or — as with these duck studies — perfectly deep and clear, its wetness on feathers so cleverly painted.

LEFT:
Fulvous tree-duck   *Dendrocygna bicolor*
oil   22.9 x 35.6 cm   (9 x 14")   1980

RIGHT:
Ringed teal   *Callonetta leucophrys*
oil   30.5 x 40.6 cm   (12 x 16")   1978

This painting of a plate-billed mountain toucan is unusual in that it was painted in just two afternoons from a living bird in a zoological collection. It is quite common for Ray to draw from birds held in zoos, but unusual for the completed painting to be carried out on the spot. Usually, only drawings will be made on 'location' and these are then transferred to the final canvas or wood panel back in the studio. Only then will the final details of plumage and the birds' exact patterns and colours be made from the artist's cabinet study-skins.

Nobody knows the precise function of the thin yellow panels or plates that run along the sides of the toucan's beak, but what is apparent is that on each individual bird, they follow a slightly different line and shape, rather like fingerprints.

ABOVE:
Cattle egret   *Bubulcus ibis*   oil on panel   23.5 x 36.2 cm   (9¼ x 14¼")   undated

NEAR RIGHT:
Toucans   pencil   47 x 33.7 cm   (18½ x 13¼")   undated

FAR RIGHT:
Plate-billed mountain toucan   *Andigena laminirostris*   oil on panel   48.3 x 35.6cm   (19 x 14")   1978

RIGHT:
The gumdigger's waistcoat
North Island brown kiwi   *Apteryx australis mantelli*
oil   48.9 x 43.2 cm   (19¼ x 17")   1969

LEFT:
North Island brown kiwi   *A. australis mantelli*
oil   50.8 x 61 cm   (20 x 24")   undated

From the earliest times in Harris-Ching's life, images of kiwis were there — the dominant bird in his childhood. They were depicted on coins and banknotes; they identified New Zealand products. Kiwis were seen on tins of polish and souvenir tea towels as 'comic' members of the animal kingdom — seemingly disadvantaged by being unable to fly and nearly blind. With their nostrils on the tip of their beaks and their oversized eggs laid in dark, damp burrows on the forest floor, kiwis were not to be taken too seriously.

Now, years later, Harris-Ching clearly perceives this extraordinary creature as one of the most wonderful and intriguing of all the birds he has painted. Indeed, only recently have conditions to study and draw kiwis so improved that it is now possible for detailed drawings to be made directly from living birds. Even the skills of the great Victorian bird illustrators were usually insufficient to overcome the lack of information available to them and with kiwis more than any other bird (so little do they look and behave like any other) this was apparent in the quality of the finished work. Ray Harris-Ching has certainly been the first to overcome this and in *New Zealand Birds* he has drawn kiwis, for the first time, behaving quite naturally. The studies of birds feeding are especially interesting and for a monograph on the *Apteryx* species, he has prepared further unique plates of kiwis nesting, feeding and even fighting.

LEFT:
Mitre Peak   mixed waterbased media on paper   30.5 x 47.6 cm   (12 x 18¾")   1984

BELOW:
Milford Sound   sketch   acrylic on paper   28.2 x 34.9 cm   (11⅛ x 13¾")   1984

The tuatara is the last living member of a group of reptiles that preceded some dinosaurs and may have appeared, more or less, as we see it now, some 135 million years ago. Its ancestors, the Rhynchocephalia or 'beak-heads', no doubt ranged over much of our planet, but have now just this single representative of their great order, living nowhere else but on the off-shore islands of New Zealand.

LEFT:
Tuatara   *Sphenodon punctatus*
oil   21.6 x 31.1 cm   (8½ x 12¼")   1980

RIGHT:
Tuatara   *S. punctatus*
watercolour   53.3 x 35.6 cm   (21 x 14")
undated

BELOW:
New Zealand fur seal   *Arctoephalus forsteri*
pencil   27.9 x 53.3 cm   (11 x 21")   1984

Tuatara (*Sphenodon punctatus*)
male
nom. gen. showing pattern of white
spots under neck.

raymond ching

The introduction, primarily for settler's hedgerows, of the gorse plant into colonial New Zealand is regretted perhaps more than any other single interference into the natural order of the islands. It has choked out more useful plants, discouraged grazing and has a generally depressing effect on the look of the land.

The largish spider *Dolomedes minor,* however, is one of the very few beneficiaries. This Arachnid has put the gorse to good use by utilising the outer branches and twigs to support its nets. The pale gauzelike nurseries, about as big as a fist, are a familiar part of both the New Zealand countryside and its domestic gardens.

LEFT:
Nursery spider   *Dolomedes minor*   oil   31.8 x 44.5 cm   (12½ x 17½")   1987

LEFT:
Black swan   *Cygnus atratus*   oil   73 x 82.6 cm   (28¾ x 32½")   1987

BELOW:
Rain near Greymouth   oil   35.6 x 45.7 cm   (14 x 18")   1984

The artist writes of this painting, that '... of the watercolours painted in recent years, this study of three sandpipers comes as close as any to saying just what I'd hoped it might'. The birds are drawn life-size and with fairly tight control exerted throughout to restrict the use of white pigment in favour of letting the texture of the white paper come through.

This same technique was employed in the fine study 'Sand dunes' made some years earlier.

ABOVE:
Sand dunes
watercolour   40 x 53.3 cm   (15¾ x 21")   1975

RIGHT:
Sharp-tailed sandpiper   *Calidris acuminata*
watercolour   (detail)   44.5 x 39.4 cm   (17½ x 15½")   1980

ABOVE:
Redbilled gull   *Larus novaehollandiae*   oil on prepared gesso panel   48.3 x 35.6 cm   (19 x 14")   1977

RIGHT:
Royal spoonbill   *Platalea regia*   pencil   53.3 x 35.6 cm   (21 x 14")   undated

FAR RIGHT ABOVE:
Black-backed gull   *Larus dominicanus*   oil   30.5 x 39.4 cm   (12 x 15½")   1985

FAR RIGHT BELOW:
Black-backed gull   *L. dominicanus*   oil   29.2 x 36.8 cm   (11½ x 14½")   1985

This painting began as a portrait of a gull but like so many of Harris-Ching's sketches finally became a study of water. Just a small piece of the sea is shown, on a coast, between rocks big enough for the artist to climb about on. Harris-Ching has worked at showing the kelp and other weeds, barely under the surface, swirling this way and that with the tide.

Pacific gulls breed on islands and headlands along the southern coasts of Australia, from Sydney in the east to Shark Bay in Western Australia. Adults, in particular, are sedentary birds and this gull species is rarely seen inland.

In appearance, the mature bird is similar to the more widespread southern black-backed gull, but is considerably larger (in fact, it is the largest Australian gull) and the bird has a noticeably deep bill with a pronounced and indeed unique oval shape to the nostrils.

LEFT:
Wave study watercolour
61 x 52.7 cm   (24 x 20¾")   1976

RIGHT:
Pacific gull   *Larus pacificus*
oil on panel   48.3 x 35.6 cm   (19 x 14")   1981

In forested areas over much of south-eastern Australia, koalas can be seen without too much effort, usually just the one — or perhaps a pair — located best by looking for the bump on a high branch that seems not quite to fit in line with the rest of the tree. Not all eucalypts offer leaves suitable to the koala's diet but when the animals do find a suitable stand, they seldom come to ground to venture far, or indeed, leave the trees at all.

This, the most familiar of Australian animals, is seen afresh in the many sheets of oil and pencil studies that are accumulating in the artist's studio — a consequence of several extensive field-trips over recent years — and are, so very much, an indication of his increasing interest in the extraordinary fauna of this continent.

The closely observed attitudes of young koalas are part of a series of pencil studies that represent an intriguing new appraisal of how these animals actually look — as opposed to the clichéd 'storybook' images which for so long have been accepted as reality.

ABOVE:
Koala   studies of young and an adult   *P. cinereus*
pencil   48.3 x 75 cm   (19 x 29½")   1984

RIGHT:
Koala   adults and young   *Phascolarctos cinereus*
oil   55.9 x 44.5 cm   (22 x 17½")   1984

RIGHT:
Young koala   *Phascolarctos cinereus*   oil   47 x 35.6 cm   (18½ x 14")   1987

The startling study opposite of a blue-winged kookaburra is a painting that appears deceptively simple in structure; nevertheless, the work is very tightly controlled and extremely complex. In earlier paintings of laughing kookaburras, Harris-Ching had not resolved how to convey, so perfectly, the underlying energy of these large kingfishers.

ABOVE
Laughing kookaburra   *Dacelo novaeguineae*   oil   25.4 x 39.4 cm   (10 x 15½")   arched top   1987

RIGHT:
Blue-winged kookaburra   *D. leachii*   oil on panel   50.8 x 38.7 cm   (20 x 15¼")   1987

More than perhaps any other country, Australia has inspired Harris-Ching's interest in painting landscapes. From a puzzled initial encounter with this seemingly monotonous landscape, often sparsely vegetated, he began to attune his eye to the variety of delicate grey-green shades of gum trees and to the ancient rock formations amid a landscape alive with the rustling, flutter and movement of animal life. Above all, he became fascinated by the vast background of spaciousness so easily able to reduce animals to tiny pinpricks of life when seen against its hugely dramatic scale.

RIGHT:
Cockatoos at Hall's Gap   oil   55.9 x 66 cm   (22 x 26")   1984-87

LEFT:
Red-tailed black cockatoo *Calyptorhynchus magnificus*
pencil   53.3 x 35.6 cm   (21 x 14")   1980

ABOVE:
Letter-wing kites   *Elanus scriptus*
pencil   53.3 x 35.6 cm   (21 x 14")   1980

RIGHT:
Long-billed corella   *Cacatua tenuirostris*
pencil   50.8 x 35.6 cm   (20 x 14")   1980

ABOVE:
Sulphur-crested cockatoo   *Cacatua galerita*   oil on panel   37.5 x 49.5 cm   (14¾ x 19½")   1987

RIGHT:
Wedge-tailed eagle (and cockatoo)   *Aquila audax*   oil   90.2 x 77.5 cm   (35½ x 30½")   1987

The short bill and unusual head shape give a curiously gooselike silhouette to this otherwise unremarkable duck. Indeed, the bird was formerly known as the maned goose, and has been variously thought to be connected to shelducks or pigmy geese and the Carolina duck. Whatever the bird's origin, the painter's interest in this small oil sketch lies as much with watery habitat as with the bird itself.

Much the same can be said of the three pencil studies of moorhens which are among the most elaborate and perfectly finished of any of the 200 or so sheets of drawings brought back from recent field-trips.

RIGHT:
Dusky moorhens   *Gallinula tenebrosa*
pencil   53.3 x 61 cm   (21 x 24")   1984

BELOW:
Maned duck   *Chenonetta jubata*
oil   21.6 x 44.5 cm   (8½ x 17½")   1984

The date, 1983-87, assigned to this painting is unusual. The red kangaroo has always struck Ray as such a beautifully splendid animal that, for years, he hardly dared to paint it and once begun, this work stood about in the workrooms in an unfinished state for three years — a rare period of deliberation for the artist. Visitors to his studio over the period were struck by the presence of this huge drawing — the brooding patience (or is it resignation?) of the animal always evoked a feeling of admiration and sympathy in the viewer. Harris-Ching responded to their comments by expressing an anxiety that the final painting would never be any better than the drawing and in fact, when pressed, he admitted to a nervousness about proceeding that was forcing him into a stop-start approach of an almost destructive nature. Completed, the work can be seen as one of his strongest animal paintings and carries absolutely not a sign of the doubts and fears that plagued its creation.

LEFT:
Red kangaroo *Macropus rufus* oil on canvas 66 x 122 cm (26 x 48") 1983-87

Harris-Ching has said that he finds, '... these great marsupials hard to separate from the land — so much do they look like its line and colour. Their spirit and presence seem so exactly to reflect the vast passages of time especially felt in the centre of this huge place.' He sees this painting as a merging of his images of kangaroos, real and pictorial — culled equally from encounters in the wild where the gentle beauty of this animal has so impressed him, and from commercial images seen so frequently on road signs and tourist maps.

Apart from the closely worked head, the painting displays a looseness of style unusual in his output, but he has nonetheless taken pains to show (from the touches of grey and the larger head proportions) that this is a young animal.

Harris-Ching is never afraid to let art take precedence over nature if the need arises and in this painting he is well aware that the upright attitude is not strictly correct. A running kangaroo usually appears more hunched over, but Ray wanted this young animal to display an air of vigour and innocence, untouched as yet by human harassment.

The flock of corellas in the lower panel was painted after a memorable sighting of these beautiful birds against an evening sky near Hamilton in Victoria, where apparently the only flocks remaining of this species are still seen.

Brother, the Great Spirit made us all.
RED JACKET, SENECA INDIAN, 1792

ABOVE:
Red kangaroo   *M. rufus*   oil on panel   25.4 x 40.6 cm   (10 x 16")   1984

RIGHT:
'Brother, the Great Spirit made us all ...', young red kangaroo and corellas   diptych
oil   upper panel   87.6 x 94 cm   (34½ x 37")   lower panel   14.6 x 94 cm   (5¾ x 37")   1987

The crested bronzewing is one of Australia's most striking pigeons and one that may have benefited from the European presence in Australia, finding as it does much of its food among cultivated crops and introduced weeds.

When landing, these birds characteristically swing their tail well above the body in a movement that somehow reflects the shape of the sharp, pointed crest. It comes as no surprise that the bird's elegant build has attracted the artist to draw and paint the species repeatedly.

Common bronzewings are usually seen feeding in pairs or perhaps in small flocks at the roadside, particularly in the early morning and again in the late afternoon. Where the cover is good, bronzewings will spend much of their time on the ground, but are wary birds and will immediately fly off at the slightest indication of danger.

LEFT:
Common bronzewing   *Phaps chalcoptera*
pencil   50.8 x 35.6 cm   (20 x 14")   1980

RIGHT:
Crested pigeon   *Ocyphaps lophotes*
pencil   53.3 x 35.6 cm   (21 x 14")   1980

These studies of Australian pigeons are among the most subtle and refined bird paintings the artist has yet completed. Indeed, his study of the courtship of a pair of common bronzewings (see page 175) is widely recognised as a milestone in contemporary bird art. Less dramatic but still nonetheless charming, the smaller painting below shows a solitary female standing quietly in fallen leaves under gums, looking as though she herself might be made of leaves and light. Note the blades of fresh grass pushing through the forest litter and of a green that exactly mimics the flash of bronze-green on her wing.

BELOW:
Common bronzewing   *Phaps chalcoptera*
oil on panel   30.5 x 43.2 cm   (12 x 17")   1981

RIGHT:
Crested pigeon   *Ocyphaps lophotes*
oil   61 x 45.7 cm   (24 x 18")   detail   1980

RIGHT:
Courtship   common bronzewings   oil   61 x 45.7 cm   (24 x 18")   1981

This study of eucalypt branches was drawn on a day's outing near Melbourne and was almost certainly intended either as a pre-study or more likely as the 'underdrawing' for a painting. The pencil is drawn directly on to a gessoed panel and is especially interesting in that it shows the extent of preparatory drawing underneath a typical finished painting of this size.

ABOVE:
Magpie goose   *Anseranas semipalmata*
oil   44.5 x 31.8 cm   (17½ x 12½")   1984

RIGHT:
Eucalypt branches study
pencil   45.7 x 76.8 cm   (18 x 30¼")   1985

These studies of crows and ravens, along with the pair of straw-necked ibis, show Harris-Ching's continuing interest in both the splendour and diversity of glossy plumage and reflect his quite obsessive curiosity with the surface of things. The artist's dilemma remains the challenge of capturing the tenuous facets of light by means of solid and permanent strokes of paint.

ABOVE:
Straw-necked ibis *Threskiornis spinicollis* oil on panel 53.3 x 38.1 cm (21 x 15") 1981

ABOVE RIGHT:
Australian crows and ravens oil on card 53.3 x 39.4 cm (21 x 15½") 1981

RIGHT:
Southern cassowary (immature) *Casuarius casuarius* oil on panel 48.3 x 35.6 cm (19 x 14") 1980

ABOVE:
Darter   *Anhinga melanogaster*   oil on panel   43.2 x 34.3 cm   (17 x 13½")   1981

RIGHT:
Darter   *A. melanogaster*   pencil   36.8 x 53.3 cm   (14½ x 21")   1981

LEFT:
Red-necked pademelon *Thylogale thetis*
oil 35.6 x 60 cm (14 x 23½") 1985

BELOW:
Australian pelican *Pelecanus conspicillatus*
pencil 50.8 x 35.6 cm (20 x 14") 1980

The red-necked pademelon is one of three species of pademelon — the other two being the red-legged and the Tasmanian. These medium to smallish marsupials are related to wallabies and, typically, all are found in areas of wet forest with a range restricted to the eastern coastal strip of Australia and the islands of Tasmania and New Guinea.

The red-necked pademelon is probably the most familiar and, indeed, in some places populations may from time to time reach plague proportions. The animals favour forest fringes, especially those adjacent to pasture or grassland.

The pademelons are timid creatures, seldom venturing far from cover, and are well known for their habit of making runways through vegetation which they use in the evenings on their way to grazing places and in the mornings on their return. Here they are shown taking refuge from the noon sun, among boulders.

Often the first sighting of this huge eagle may be of a pair soaring high in the sky, pursued by a number of magpies.

Males are slightly smaller than females, but are still very large and extremely impressive — in fact, they are one of the world's largest eagles, and certainly one of the most splendid. The wedge-shaped tail looks long and distinctive and in flight, with its great wings stretched to a V-shape, the silhouette is unmistakable.

When prey is sighted (often birds and reptiles, but creatures as large as young kangaroos are taken), wedgetails fold their wings and fall steeply upon their victims. Their killing effectiveness is often increased by their habit of hunting in pairs.

LEFT:
Wedge-tailed eagle   *Aquila audax*
pencil   50.8 x 35.6 cm   (20 x 14")   1981

RIGHT:
Wedge-tailed eagle   *A. audax*
watercolour   71.1 x 50.8 cm   (28 x 20")   1981

Nine times out of ten, when your attention is attracted by the hop-hopping of this tiny, brilliantly coloured, blue and black bird, a second or third look will reveal his mate, subtly patterned in palish brown with creamy underparts.

After the breeding season, males 'eclipse' into a plumage very similar to the female's, but they retain, among other small differences, a delicate blue wash on their tails.

LEFT:
Superb blue wren *Malurus cyaneus*
oil   39.4 x 50.2 cm   (15½ x 19¾")   1984

RIGHT:
Superb blue wren   *M. cyaneus*
pencil   50.8 x 33 cm   (20 x 13")   1981

RIGHT:
Platypus *Ornithorhynchus anatinus* oil on panel 42 x 50.8 cm (16 ½ x 20") 1985

LEFT:
Platypus studies   pencil   53.3 x 61 cm   (21 x 24")   undated

ABOVE:
Platypus   *Ornithorhynchus anatinus*   pencil   22.9 x 35.6 cm   (9 x 14")   undated

Curiously, when swimming underwater, platypuses can neither see nor hear and navigate instead by their extremely sensitive bills! Both ears and eyes are housed in a single deep groove on either side of the head and are tightly closed when underwater. The problems of painting an animal in motion that appears 'blind' are neatly overcome here by the artist making the most of the dark shadows in this groove that finally give the appearance of an animal's eye.

LEFT:
Platypus   *Ornithorhynchus anatinus*
oil   91.4 x 77.5 cm   (36 x 30½")   1987

Platypuses first came to European attention with the settlement of Australia and it wasn't long before suspicions were voiced that this extraordinary mammal laid eggs. This proved such a revolutionary and totally surprising concept that the issue was only resolved following decades of argument.

Perhaps the most immediately obvious peculiarity of this aquatic animal is its large, dark, duck-like bill. When the first preserved specimens reached Europe in the very last years of the eighteenth century, naturalists suspected a hoax, and believed that the bill was the result of some human artifice — a bird's beak stuck on to the body of some hitherto unknown otter-like animal!

The platypus is quite common in suitable riverbank environments in eastern and southeastern Australia, but such is their nature that they are rarely seen unless sought out.

Mixed flocks of these smallish birds (commonly the black-faced and the dusky woodswallow) present themselves readily to the artist's gaze, often quite close to roadsides perhaps among low bushes, and it's a simple fact that birds offering the best and closest view will, most usually, make the best pictures.

Harris-Ching has clearly felt confident (as a consequence, no doubt, of the many sheets of closely detailed pencil studies he has made of these wild creatures) of producing a tightly resolved, highly finished painting; he is so often at his best when structuring a work as simply and as clearly as this. Not a line could be added or taken away without disturbing the whole, and he is able to say what he wants in such a straight-forward and direct way.

There are ten species of woodswallows, six of which are Australian, the other four from the South Pacific, the Philippines and India. Although the family is classed as a passerine, its relationship to other passerine groups is obscure. The woodswallow's closest relatives may be the waxwings, but this is far from certain; what is clear is that despite their name they are in no way related to any kind of swallow.

With its subtle grey and white markings and its striking black mask, the black-faced woodswallow is found in large numbers in the drier parts of Australia but is replaced by the dusky woodswallow along the eastern and south-eastern coastal strip; this species also occurs in parts of New Guinea.

LEFT:
Black-faced woodswallow   *Artamus cinereus*
pencil studies   53.3 x 35.6 cm   (21 x 14")
undated

RIGHT:
Black-faced woodswallow   *A. cinereus*
oil on panel   48.3 x 35.6 cm   (19 x 14")   1982
undated

There is not, Harris-Ching says, even in his imagination, a more complex and subtly patterned bird than the mysteriously beautiful lyrebird. One may puzzle over the lack of fine paintings of this bird — the species should be one of the world's great inspirations to a bird painter — but when Harris-Ching began work on this picture, his first of the species, he quickly discovered why the bird is so seldom depicted. To render the subtle tracery of the male's tail, which seems so exactly to reflect the delicate lines and fragile colours of its forest floor habitat, proved one of the most difficult technical problems the artist had encountered.

Almost as marvellous as the bird's appearance are its calls that mimic the creatures whose habitat it shares — kookaburras, cockatoos, bowerbirds, whipbirds, whistlers, etc. 'But best of all,' the painter says, 'is the ssh, ssh, ssh of its tail, framed over the bird's head and shimmering in display — a sound as thin and as dry as the crackle of fallen gum leaves under its feet.'

ABOVE:
Lyrebird (female)　　*Menura superba*　　pencil　　48.3 x 73.7 cm　　(19 x 29")　　undated

RIGHT:
Lyrebird　　*M. superba*　　oil　　59.7 x 85.1 cm　　(23½ x 33½")　　1987

The musk duck must surely be one of the strangest of all waterfowl with its heavily musk-scented, pendulous lobe of dark skin hanging from the throat. The grotesque silhouette is peculiar to the males, although both adults share the same dark, near black plumage, and both carry themselves very low in the water. Indeed, if disturbed or frightened, they may sink so low as to leave only their eyes and beak above the surface.

These are truly aquatic birds, refusing normally to come ashore at all, but if by some circumstance they do find themselves on land, they flop and slide about, quite unable to maintain the 'usual' upright duck posture.

ABOVE:
Green pygmy goose   *Nettapus puchellus*
pencil   53.3 x 36.2 cm   (21 x 14¼")   1981

RIGHT:
Musk duck   *Biziura lobata*
oil   32.4 x 45.1 cm   (12¾ x 17¾")   1987

for Chris, with love Rowland
(after Norman Lindsay's etching "Trump?
and their love") *Vombatus hirsutus*

Similar in size and texture to a large doormat, the common wombat is similarly dusty and often not a great deal more mobile! They are, nonetheless, endearing animals that have been the subject of many of Harris-Ching's drawings, of which this large study is one of the most entertaining.

LEFT:
'The Wild Things have their Hour'
wombat   *Vombatus hirsuitus*
pencil   48.3 x 73.7 cm   (19 x 29")   1985

Fire plays such a significant role in the natural order that landscapes often show the impact of its presence in ways sometimes obvious, sometimes less so. Hulks of burned trees stand above tops of newly generated bush and forest growth, making the distinctive silhoutte that is so characteristically Australian. Here, Harris-Ching shows a restless flycatcher just ahead of fire, fluttering above the heat that will drive out the insect life which forms such a important part of the bird's diet.

LEFT:
Restless flycatcher   *Myiagra inquieta*
oil   68.6 x 53.3 cm   (27 x 21")   undated

RIGHT:
Grey butcherbird   *Cracticus torquatus*
oil   66 x 53.3 cm   (26 x 21")   detail   undated

As a boy growing up in New Zealand's North Island, with over 1600 kilometres of sea separating him from the great landmass of Australia, Ray would watch, blowing nearer and nearer, great palls of smoke originating from some huge bush fire ravaging the east coast of Australia. He wondered how anything could survive fire on such a scale, not then understanding how fire is one of the central forces governing the natural order on the continent and that many plants and animals have evolved life-styles and breeding cycles that rely upon fire for success.

LEFT:
Zebra finches   *Poephila guttata*
acrylic and oil   64.8 x 99.1 cm   (25 ½ x 39")
undated

Goannas, and indeed most lizards, are among the best wild animal models for the painter because under the right circumstances they will remain very still for very long periods. It may sound unexciting to reveal that often an animal that habitually moves slower and less readily than another will be the one selected to be drawn, but this simple fact does bear heavily on the range of subjects that a painter may depict. All wild things are more or less beautiful, and so the ones that will allow the artist time for consideration and perhaps detailed drawing will often be among those most often chosen to be painted.

These pratincoles are quite common birds over much of Australia's harsh interior, where they breed in the very hot summer months in temperatures regularly above 50° Centigrade! The birds construct no nest, but rather simply lay two pale buff eggs on the bare ground in the full blaze of the sun, sometimes surrounding the site with a decorative ring of stones. The parent birds make only the slightest concession to the heat, each taking turns to cool down by moving to a nearby rise or rock where the temperature may be slightly lower, and once the chicks are hatched, the adults will lead them off to the cover of, perhaps, a hole under boulders, where they can shelter from the worst excesses of the heat.

LEFT:
Australian pratincole   *Stiltia isabella*
oil   40.6 x 30.5 cm   (16 x 12")   1980

RIGHT:
Goannas
pencil   40 x 50.2 cm   (15¾ x 19¾")   1983

Goanna
(genus *Varanus*)

ABOVE: Crocodile   oil   27.9 x 20.3 cm   (11 x 8")   1982

ABOVE: Crocodile   oil on panel   27.9 x 20.3 cm   (11 x 8")   1982

For many years the painter's feelings about the spiny-cheeked honeyeater were that, although not unattractive, it was nevertheless not interesting enough to form the subject of a painting. It was not until a chance 'close encounter' with an adult — which popped up on a branch supporting a group of caterpillars being sketched — that Ray was able to see in detail its finely marked and very delicate plumage. At that moment the seeds for this lovely watercolour were sown. He writes, 'The curious bi-coloured bill makes these birds truly distinctive, but as much as anything, it is their eyes, a delicate shade of blue, that for me set the pale, slightly faded feel of this watercolour.'

Begun in 1981 on a field-trip in Victoria, the more or less completed birds had to wait until the painter's return to Australia in 1985 for the addition of the gum leaves and the eventual resolution of the composition.

RIGHT:
Spiny-cheeked honeyeater   *Acanthagenys rufogularis*   watercolour   57.2 x 50.8 cm (22½ x 20")   1981-85

Exhibitions

1966 *Thirty Birds,* John Leech Gallery, Auckland, New Zealand.
1967 *Studies of New Zealand Wildlife,* John Leech Gallery, Auckland, New Zealand.
1970 *Pencil drawings from The Book of British Birds,* Tryon Gallery, London, England.
1972 *Bird Artists of the World,* The Tryon Gallery, London, England (group exhibition).
1974 *Bird Books and Bird Art,* The Moorland Gallery, London, England (group exhibition).
1975 *Endangered Species,* The Tryon Gallery, London, England (group exhibition).
1976 *Drawings,* The Falcon Gallery, Auckland, New Zealand.
Pieter Wenning Gallery/Tryon Gallery, South Africa (group exhibition).
1977 *Jubilee Exhibition,* The Tryon & Moorland Galleries, London, England (group exhibition).
Recent Paintings & Drawings, Rye Art Gallery, Rye, England.
Paintings & Drawings, International Art Centre, Auckland, New Zealand.
1979 *Society of Animal Artist's Exhibition,* Sportsman's Edge/Explorer's Club, U.S.A. (group exhibition).
Birds in Art Exhibition, Leigh Yawkey Woodson Art Museum, Wasau, U.S.A. (group exhibition).
1980 *Birds in Art Exhibition,* Leigh Yawkey Woodson Art Museum, Wasau, U.S.A. (group exhibition).
Paintings, International Art Centre, Auckland New Zealand.
1981 *Tryon & Moorland Artists' Major Wildlife Exhibition,* Tryon Gallery, London, England (group exhibition).
Society of Animal Artist's Exhibition, Academy of Natural Sciences, Philadelphia, U.S.A. (group exhibition).
1982 *Bird Paintings & Sketches,* Tryon & Moorland Gallery, London, England.
Paintings & Drawings, International Art Centre, Auckland, New Zealand.
Birds in Art Exhibition, Leigh Yawkey Woodson Art Museum, Wasau, U.S.A. (group exhibition).
1983 *Birds in Art Exhibition,* Leigh Yawkey Woodson Art Museum, Wasau, U.S.A. (group exhibition).
1984 *Bird Artists of the World,* Everard Read Gallery/The Tryon Gallery, Johannesburg, South Africa (group exhibition)
1985 *Birds in Art Exhibition,* Leigh Yawkey Woodson Art Museum, Wasau, U.S.A. (group exhibition).
Wildlife Art Society of Australasia, Melbourne, Australia (group exhibition).
Wildlife Artists of the World, Johannesburg, South Africa (group exhibition).
Collector's Covey, Dallas, U.S.A. (group exhibition).
1986 *The Gilded Triptych & Recent Wildlife Paintings,* The Tryon & Moorland Gallery, London, England.
Birds in Art Exhibition, Leigh Yawkey Woodson Art Museum, Wasau, U.S.A. (group exhibition).
Everard Read/Stremmel Gallery, U.S.A. (group exhibition).
Nature in Art, Society of Wildlife Art for the Nations, London, England, (group exhibition).
1987 *Wildlife in Art,* Leigh Yawkey Woodson Art Museum, (travelling group exhibition, 1987-1989) U.S.A.
1988 *Wild Portraits,* Rye Art Gallery, Rye, England.
Wild Portraits, The Tryon & Moorland Gallery, London, England.
Wild Portraits, The Australian Galleries/The Tryon Gallery, Melbourne, Australia.

Bibliography

Buch Der Vogelwelt, Stuttgart, 1973,

El Libra De Las Aves De Espana, Madrid, 1972.

Guide Des Oiseaux, Paris-Zurich, 1971.

HAMMOND, Nicholas, *Twentieth Century Wildlife Artists,* Croom Helm, London, 1986.

HANSARD, Peter, *The Art of Raymond Ching,* Collins, Auckland, 1981.

———, *The Art of Raymond Ching,* Alpine Fine Arts, New York, 1982.

HARRIS-CHING, Raymond, *New Zealand Birds, An Artist's Field-Studies,* Reed Methuen, Auckland, 1986.

———, *Studies & Sketches of a Bird Painter,* Lansdowne, Melbourne, 1981.

———, *Studies & Sketches of a Bird Painter,* Lansdowne, (limited edition 500 copies), Melbourne, 1981

———, *Studies & Sketches of a Bird Painter,* Abrams, New York, 1981.

Het Beste Vogelboek, Amsterdam, 1971, 1972.

Norges Fugleliv, Oslo, 1971.

Nya Fagel Boken, Stockholm, 1970.

RAYFIELD, Susan, *Painting Birds,* Watson Guptill, New York, 1988.

———, *Wildlife Painting, Techniques of Modern Masters,* Watson Guptill, New York, 1985.

The Reader's Digest A.A. Book of British Birds, Reader's Digest, London, 1969, 1970, 1972, 1974, 1977, 1980, 1983, 1986.

SNOW, David, A. H. CHISHOLM, and M. F. SOPER, *The Bird Paintings,* Collins, London, 1978.

———, *The Bird Paintings, Watercolour and Pencil Drawings 1969-1975,* Collins (with a special coloured frontispiece, bound by Zaehnsdorf, limited edition 350 copies), London, 1978.

———, *The Bird Paintings,* Collins (limp edition), Auckland, 1984, 1985.

Valitut Palat Lintukirja, Helsinki, 1971, 1973.

Index

African eagle-owl 41
American kestrel *(Falco sparverius)* 100-01
American widgeon *(Anas americana)* 111
Anna's hummingbird *(Calypte anna)* 38, 108
Armoury, The 27, 28
Armoury library 26
Asian hornbill 41
Australian crows and ravens 178
Australian pelican *(Pelecanus conspicillatus)* 183
Australian pratincole *(Stiltia isabella)* 206
Australian wildlife painting 19-21

Bald eagle *(Haliaeetus leucocephalus)* 44, 104-05
Barn owl *(Tyto alba)* 9, 97
Bateman, Robert 23
Bears 63, 107
Bee *(Bombus locorum)* 80-81
Black and white casqued hornbill *(Bycanistes subcylindricus)* 41, 51-53
Black bear *(Ursus)* 63
Black swan *(Cygnus atratus)* 144
Blackbirds 24, 42-43, 46
Black-backed gull *(Larus dominicanus)* 148
Black-capped chickadee 38
Black-crowned night heron *(Nycticorax nycticorax)* 109, 212
Black-faced woodswallow *(Artamus cinereus)* 193-94
Blue jay *(Cyanocitta cristata)* 38
Blue-winged kookaburra *(Dacelo leachii)* 156-57
Botany Bay 19
Brambles 86
Brewer's blackbirds 42-43
Bronzewings 170-72, 175
'Brother, the Great Spirit made us all' 169
Brush-turkey *(Alectura lathami)* 22
Butcherbirds 203
Buzzards 38, 94-95

Camel study   frontispiece
Canvasback *(Aythya valisineria)* 111
Caracal *(Felis caracal)* 58-59
Cassowaries 179
Cattle egret *(Bubulcus ibis)* 39, 134
Chickadee 38
Chimpanzee *(Pan troglodytes)* 62
Charley Barley 18
Cockatoos 39, 158-60, 162
Cockatoos at Hall's Gap 158-59
Common bronzewing *(Phaps chalcoptera)* 170-72, 175
Common shrew *(Sorex araneus)* 66-67
Common squirrel monkey *(Saimiri sciureus)* 130-31
Corellas 161, 169
Courtship 175
Crane 41
Crested pigeon *(Ocyphaps lophotes)* 171-73
Crested porcupine *(Hystrix cristata)* 62
Crested screamer *(Chauna torquata)* 41
Crocodiles 208-09
Crows 178

Darter *(Anhinga melanogaster)* 180-81
Desert falcon studies 57
Diana monkey *(Cercopithecus diana)* 12
Domestic duck 70-71
Domestic fowls and chicks 117
Domestic rabbits 116
Doves 42-43, 102-03
Ducks 32, 44-45, 70-71, 78, 110, 164, 198-99
Dusky moorhens *(Gallinula tenebrosa)* 164-65

Eagles 39, 44, 99, 104-05, 163, 184-85
Echidna in the Grampian Mountains 21
Egrets 39, 134
Eucalypt branches study 176-77
European blackbird *(Turdus merula)* 24, 46

European buzzard *(Buteo buteo)* 38, 94-95
European hare *(Lepus europaeus)* 98
European kingfisher *(Alcedo atthis)* 72-73
European robin *(Erithacus rubecula)* 68-69
European sparrowhawk *(Accipiter nisus)* 96-97

Falcons 39, 56-57
Finches 114, 205
Flycatchers 202
Frogmouths 23
Fulvous tree-duck *(Dendrocygna bicolor)* 132

Geese 176, 198
Gilded Triptych, The 28-48
Glossy starling 39
Goannas 206-07
Goldcrest *(Regulus regulus)* nest 80
Golden eagle *(Aquila chrysaetos)* 39, 99
Grasses 89
Green peacock 41
Green pygmy goose *(Nettapus pulchellus)* 198
Grey butcherbird *(Cracticus torquatus)* 203
Grey partridge *(Perdix perdix)* 25, 84, 87, 115
Guillemots 28
Gulls 7, 148, 150-51
Gumdigger's waistcoat, The 137

Hares 98
Harris-Ching, Ray: in the crypt, 29; in the studio, 16; in the You-Yangs, 20; influences, 27-28; interest in Australian fauna, 19-21; painting techniques, 25-28; studios, 21-23; study sketches, 21
Harris hawk 38
Herons 5, 41, 109
Honey-eaters 14, 210-11
Hornbills 41, 42-43, 51-53

215

House sparrow *(Passer domesticus)*   42-43, 44-45, 64-65, 82
Hummingbirds   38, 108

Ibis   39, 41, 178

Japanese crane   41
Java sparrow   38
Jays   38

Kangaroos   166-69
Kestrels   100-01
King vulture *(Sarcogyps calvus)*   41
Kingfishers   72-73
Kites   160-61
Kittiwake *(Rissa tridactyla)*   106
Kiwis   136-37
Koala *(Phascolarctos cinereus)*   152-155
Kookaburras   156-57

Laughing kookaburra *(Dacelo novaeguineae)*   156
Letter-wing kites *(Elanus scriptus)*   160-61
Lion *(Panthera leo)*   60-61
Little owl *(Athene noctua)*   74-75
Long-billed corella *(Cacatua tenuirostris)*   161
Long-tailed tit *(Aegithalos caudatus)*   85
Lyrebird *(Menura superba)*   196-97

Macaque   120-21
Magpie goose *(Anseranas semipalmata)*   176
Mallard *(Anas platyrhynchos)*   70
Mandarin duck *(Aix galericulata)*   78
Maned duck *(Chenonetta jubata)*   164
McEvey, Allan   21
McLean, George   23
Milford Sound   139
Mitre Peak   138-39
Monkeys   12, 130-31
Moorhen *(Gallinula chloropus)*   85, 164-65
Mourning doves *(Zenaidura macroura)*   42-43, 102-03
Musk duck *(Biziura lobata)*   198-99

Nest of goldcrest   80
New Zealand fur seal *(Arctoephalus forsteri)*   140-41
Night heron   41
Nilgai *(Boselaphus tragocamelus)*   122-23
North American waders   33
North Island brown kiwi *(Apteryx australis mantelli)*   136-37
Nursery spider *(Dolomedes minor)*   142-43

Otter *(Lutra lutra)*   119
Owls   9, 39, 74-75, 97, 130

Pacific gull *(Larus pacificus)*   7, 150-51
Pademelons   182-83
Parakeets   48
Partridges   25, 84, 87, 115
Peacock   41
Pelicans   183
Peregrine *(Falco peregrinus)*   41, 101
Pheasant *(Phasianus colchicus)*   87
Philippine mallard   44-45
Pigeons   171-73
Pink cockatoo   39
Plate-billed mountain toucan *(Andigena laminirostris)*   134-35
Platypus *(Ornithorhynchus anatinus)*   11, 188-93
Plumed tree-ducks   39, 41
Pochard *(Aythya ferina)*   35, 79, 112-13
Polar bear *(Thalarctos maritimus)*   107
Porcupines   62
Pratincoles   206
Purple finch *(Carpodacus purpureus)*   114

Rabbits, domestic   116
Rain near Greymouth   145
Ravens   178
Razorbill *(Alca torda)*   28, 76-77
Red kangaroo *(Macropus rufus)*   166-69
Red wattlebird *(Anthochaera carunculata)*   22
Redbilled gull *(Larus novaehollandiae)*   148
Redbilled hornbill   42-43
Red-crowned parakeet *(Cyanoramphus novaezelandiae)*   48
Redhead *(Aythya americana)*   112
Red-necked pademelon *(Thylogale thetis)*   182-83
Red-tailed black cockatoo *(Calyptorhynchus magnificus)*   160
Redwing *(Turdus iliacus)*   85
Restless flycatcher *(Myiagra inquieta)*   202
Rhea   38
Ringed teal *(Callonetta leucophrys)*   133
Robins   68-69
Royal spoonbill *(Platalea regia)*   41, 148-49
Rufous night heron *(Nycticorax caledonicus)*   5

Sacred ibis *(Threskiornis aethiopicus)*   39
Saker falcon *(Falco cherrug)*   39, 56-57
Sand dunes   146
Sandpipers   146-47
Screamer   41
Sea lion   118
Seals   140-41
Sedge warbler *(Acrocephalus schoenobaenus)*   88
Serval *(Felis serval)*   54-55
Sharp-tailed sandpiper *(Calidris acuminata)*   146-47

Shrews   66-67
Song thrush *(Turdus philomelos)*   82-83, 85
Southern cassowary *(Casuarius casuarius)*   179
Sparrows   38, 42-43, 44-45, 64-65, 82
Sparrowhawks   96-97
Spectacled owl *(Pulsatrix perspicillata)*   130
Spiders   142-43
Spiny-cheeked honeyeater *(Acanthagenys rufogularis)*   210-11
Spoonbills   41, 148-49
Starling *(Sturnus vulgaris)*   39, 85
Straw-necked ibis *(Threskiornis spinicollis)*   178
Studies of razorbill and guillemot   28
Study-skins and skeletons in the studio   28
Sulphur-crested cockatoo *(Cacatua galerita)*   162
Superb blue wren *(Malurus cyaneus)*   186-87
Superb starling   41
Swans   71, 110, 144

Takahe   44
Tawny frogmouths *(Podargus strigoides)*   23
Teals   133
Thrushes   82-83, 85
Tiger *(Panthera tigris)*   124-29
Tits   85
Toucans   41, 134-35
Tree-ducks   39, 41, 132
Triptych. *See* Gilded Triptych
Tuatara *(Sphenodon punctatus)*   140-41
Tufted duck *(Aythya fuligula)*   32, 78

Vanessa   18
Vulture   41

Warblers   88
Wattlebirds   22
Wave study watercolour   150
Wedge-tailed eagle *(Aquila audax)*   163, 184-85
Whistling swan *(Cygnus olor)*   110
White-cheeked honey-eaters *(Phylidonyris nigra)*   14
White-faced scops owl   41
Widgeons   111
'Wild things have their hour, The'   201
Wombat *(Vombatus hirsuitus)*   201
Wood duck *(Aix sponsa)*   110
Woodswallow   193-94
Wren *(Troglodytes troglodytes)*   85, 90-92
Wrens   85, 90-92, 186-87

Zebra finches *(Poephila guttata)*   205

For more information on Raymond Harris-Ching's books, prints and other publications, please direct enquiries to the appropriate agents:

In New Zealand   *SeTo Publishing Ltd*
PO Box 4028
Auckland 1

In Australia   *The Australian Galleries*
35 Derby Street
Collingwood
Victoria 3066

In Great Britain   *The Tryon & Moorland Gallery*
23/24 Cork Street
London W1X 1HB